STILL SMOKIN'

STILL SMOKIN'

More than 150 New Recipes
for Savory Smoke-Cooked Dishes

COOKSHACK

RUNNING PRESS
PHILADELPHIA • LONDON

9   8   7   6   5   4
Digit on the right indicates the number of this printing

Library of Congress Control Number: 2003096213

ISBN-10: 0-7624-1903-2
ISBN-13: 978-0-7624-1903-6

Cover illustrations and design by Bill Jones
Interior illustrations by Bill Jones
Interior design by e Bond
Edited by Janet Bukovinsky Teacher
Typography: AGaramond, Manito, and Thunderbird

This book may be ordered by mail from the publisher.
Please include $2.50 for postage and handling.
But try your bookstore first!

Running Press Book Publishers
2300 Chestnut Street Suite 200
Philadelphia, PA 19103-4371

Cookshack Sales
Toll Free: 1-800-423-0698
Fax: 580-765-2223

Visit us on the web!
www.runningpress.com
www.cookshackamerica.com

COOKSHACK, INC.

"If you can eat it, you can smoke it." That's the motto of Cookshack CEO Stuart Powell. And he's a man who understands smoked foods.

Chances are, you have already enjoyed barbecue or smoked ingredients prepared the Cookshack way. Countless restaurants use Cookshack commercial smokers for consistently superior results that keep customers coming back for more.

Home cooks can get that same great flavor using Cookshack's conveniently sized, easy-to-use smokers to turn out moist, flavorful smoked foods with a minimum of fuss. From tender slow-cooked beef and pork to cold-smoked salmon to flavorful smoked chicken, cheeses, and vegetables, the Cookshack Smokette and the Cookshack Model 50 give great results to any cook, from novice to professional chef. And thanks to Cookshack's technology, the food only tastes as if you labored over it all day.

When people say barbecue today, they usually mean meat grilled over moderate heat. That doesn't leave much time for food to absorb the flavors of the wood. Smokers, on the other hand, use a lower temperature to add deep-down flavor and tenderness to meat.

There are many kinds of smokers on the market, but Cookshack is in a class by itself. Most smokers move smoke from a slow-burning fire across food toward a chimney; the wood smoke adds flavor, but as smoky air blows over the food, moisture from the food joins the smoke on its way out the chimney. Not so with Cookshack units. Thermostatic controls allow for steady, very slow heat that cooks food to perfection. The tight construction of Cookshack smokers keeps the smoke inside, where food can slowly absorb its flavors while remaining moist. With electricity heating the woodbox, the smoldering wood chips have only one job—to make the food inside taste as rich as possible. And food stays moist even without a water pan inside.

Cookshack allows anyone to recreate the slow-cooked taste of old-fashioned pit barbecue—without the old-fashioned labor. Busy cooks can put in meat or fish or poultry, do whatever else they have to do—even away from home—and return a few hours later to find everything cooked to perfection.

The Smokette holds up to 22 pounds of meat and takes approximately an hour a pound to cook (allow 45 minutes a pound to smoke turkey). The larger Model 50 holds up to 30 pounds, depending on cut. That's large enough to please even hunters and fishermen who smoke their own game, cold-cure fish, and make their own jerky. Both models have Cookshack's high-quality construction: tough, double-walled steel with

1000° insulation that keeps the warm air in while the outside is cool enough to touch. That also makes it energy efficient, and wood efficient, too—a four-ounce log of hickory, mesquite, apple, or cherry wood will smoke 20 pounds of food. Both models are available in both black and stainless steel.

Cookshack has been manufacturing high-quality commercial smoking equipment for 40 years, and home models for about 20. But company founder Gene Ellis did not set out to make his mark this way. A hog farmer with a fondness for barbecue, Ellis was also a tinkerer. After seeing a neighbor adapt an old refrigerator as the case for a smoker, Ellis built one and liked the result. He wanted to put it to commercial use by developing a chain of barbecue restaurants, starting in Ponca City, Oklahoma. He created barbecue sauces and rubs and fine-tuned his smoker design for his restaurant and set about selling his concept. Only problem was, nobody he met in the early '60s was ready to invest in a chain of barbecue restaurants. A number of them wanted his smokers, however, so Ellis instead began providing slow-cooking barbecue equipment to restaurants and barbecue joints.

What success he had. Though the company never did get into barbecue chains, Cookshack equipment works behind the scenes at some of the best restaurants in America. It's the only smoker used at the prestigious College of Culinary Arts at Johnson and Wales University—a place that knows food!

In addition to high-quality equipment, Cookshack offers great customer service. A call to its customer service department puts the consumer in touch with someone who not only knows the equipment but also uses it. The Cookshack website gives users a virtual community of slow-smoking enthusiasts, including the Smokin' Okie, who share tips and techniques. Cookshack also produces cookbooks like *Get Smokin!* (Running Press), which is exclusively smoked food recipes. And Cookshack can ship to anywhere in the world.

Lucky for all of us, Gene Ellis couldn't get that restaurant chain off the ground. Now everyone can experience the joy of slow smoking the Cookshack way.

STILL SMOKIN'

Table of Contents

Poultry and Game Birds....65

Shellfish and Seafood........87

APPETIZERS

MESQUITE-SMOKED JALAPEÑO POPPERS

Taking the seeds and membranes out of the jalapeños removes about 90 percent of the heat, leaving a really great smoked pepper flavor. This recipe from Colonel Tommy Tompkins of the United States Air Force in San Antonio, Texas, was the winner of the 2000–2001 First Prize Award from Cookshack.

MAKES 12 APPETIZERS

12 large jalapeño peppers
½ pound crabmeat, picked over for shell fragments
1 (8-ounce) package cream cheese
¼ cup finely chopped onion
½ teaspoon garlic powder
6 strips lean, center-cut bacon

Prepare the smoker with mesquite wood to 200°F. Cut each jalapeño in half lengthwise, wearing rubber gloves if desired. Scoop out the seeds and the membranes. Drain the crabmeat well. Combine the crabmeat, cream cheese, onion, and garlic powder and mix well. Divide equally among each of the pepper halves, and put the pepper halves together. Cut the bacon strips in half, wrap around each pepper, and secure with a toothpick to keep the peppers intact. Place on the top rack of the smoker and smoke until the bacon is cooked, 1½ to 2 hours.

SMOKED STUFFED MUSHROOMS

12 large mushrooms
Olive oil
½ pound lean ground beef
3 ounces cream cheese
2 tablespoons grated mozzarella cheese
½ teaspoon salt
½ teaspoon pepper
1 teaspoon Italian seasoning
1 tablespoon chopped parsley
1½ tablespoons grated Parmesan cheese

Preheat the smoker with 1 ounce of hickory wood. Wipe the mushrooms with a damp paper towel and remove the stems. Rub the outside of the mushrooms lightly with olive oil. In a medium skillet, brown the ground beef over medium heat and drain. In a large bowl, combine the ground beef, cream cheese, mozzarella, salt, pepper, and Italian seasoning. Mix well. Stuff the mushroom caps with the meat mixture. Top with parsley and grated Parmesan. Place the mushrooms on the seafood grill, if available, and smoke-cook for 1 hour.

SMOKED SALMON CAKES WITH TWO SAUCES

This recipe was submitted by Dan Disler.

1 cup kosher salt
½ cup granulated sugar
½ cup brown sugar
1 tablespoon black pepper
1 pound salmon filet
½ cup maple syrup
½ cup sour cream
1 cup unseasoned bread crumbs
2 tablespoons hot sauce
1 small shallot, minced
Salt and pepper to taste
Vegetable oil
Cilantro, for garnish
Margarita Sauce (see page 14)
Garlic Aïoli (see page 14)

In a small bowl, combine the salt, sugars, and pepper. Rub liberally to coat both sides of the salmon. Wrap tightly in plastic wrap and then in foil. Refrigerate for 8 hours. Rinse the salmon thoroughly and let it sit in a cool, dry place until the skin is dry. Preheat the smoker to 200°F. Pour the maple syrup over the salmon to coat it. Smoke-cook the salmon for 1½ to 2 hours. Remove from the smoker and cool. Break the salmon into small pieces. Place it in a medium bowl and add the sour cream, bread crumbs, hot sauce, and shallot. Add salt and pepper to taste. Mix to combine. Form into 8 small patties. Heat a heavy skillet over medium high heat and coat the bottom with oil. Add the patties and sauté, turning once, until browned, 3 to 4 minutes per side. Garnish with cilantro and serve with Margarita Sauce and Garlic Aïoli.

Margarita Sauce

½ cup tequila
2 tablespoons lime juice
1 tablespoon minced onion
1 teaspoon minced garlic
1 tablespoon chopped cilantro
¼ cup heavy cream
¼ pound (1 stick) butter, softened
Salt and pepper to taste

In a skillet, combine the tequila, lime juice, onion, garlic, and cilantro and bring to a boil. Add the cream and simmer for about 5 minutes. Add butter and remove from heat. Stir until the sauce is smooth. Add salt and pepper to taste.

Garlic Aïoli

1 head garlic
½ cup olive oil, plus more for drizzling
Salt and pepper to taste
1 egg
1 tablespoon lemon juice
Cayenne pepper
½ cup olive oil

Preheat the oven to 350°F. Slice off the top of the garlic head to expose the cloves. Drizzle with olive oil and sprinkle with salt. Wrap in foil and bake for 1 hour or until the cloves are soft. Squeeze out the garlic and combine in a blender with the egg, lemon juice, and cayenne pepper to taste. Turn on the blender and drizzle in the oil, blending to emulsify the mixture to a mayonnaise consistency. Add salt and pepper to taste.

SAVORY SMOKED MOZZARELLA AND TOMATO CHEESECAKE

*Serve this flavorful cheesecake at room temperature as
an appetizer with tomato coulis or pesto.*

¾ pound herb-seasoned croutons (homemade or purchased), finely ground
¼ pound (1 stick) butter, melted
1½ pounds cream cheese
1½ pounds smoked mozzarella, shredded
1 teaspoon kosher salt
1 teaspoon coarsely ground black pepper
⅓ cup cornstarch
5 eggs plus 3 egg yolks
2 pounds smoked tomatoes, peeled, seeded, and diced
1 smoked sweet onion, finely diced
¼ cup chopped fresh basil
¼ cup chopped chives

Preheat the oven to 350°F. Combine the crouton crumbs and the melted butter.
Press evenly over the bottom and sides of a 12-inch springform pan. In a large mixer bowl, combine
the cream cheese, mozzarella, salt, pepper, and cornstarch and beat until completely smooth.
Add the whole eggs and egg yolks and mix until incorporated. Add the tomatoes, onion, basil,
and chives. Fold in lightly. Pour the mixture into the prepared springform pan.
Bake for 2½ to 3 hours, until set. Cool before removing the sides of the pan. Cover and refrigerate
until ready to serve. Remove from the refrigerator 15 minutes before serving.

SMOKED CREAM OF TOMATO SOUP

3 pounds ripe tomatoes
⅓ cup chopped bacon
¼ pound carrots, finely chopped
¼ pound celery, finely chopped
½ cup finely chopped onion
2 tablespoons minced garlic
3 cups flour
1 quart chicken stock
2 cups light cream
Popcorn, for garnish
Fresh basil, thinly sliced, for garnish

Preheat the smoker to 225°F with 1 ounce of pecan wood. Cut each tomato in half and remove the seeds. Place the tomato halves, cut side down, on the smoker grill, and smoke-cook for 1 hour. Remove from the smoker, peel away the skins, and chop the tomatoes.

In a large saucepan, cook the bacon over medium heat. As soon as the fat begins to render, add the carrots, celery, and onion. Sauté just until the onions are translucent. Add the garlic and cook for 1 minute. Stir in the flour and cook for 2 to 3 minutes. Add the chicken stock, whisking until smooth. Add the chopped smoked tomatoes, reduce the heat to low, and simmer for 1 hour. Remove from heat and carefully puree in a food processor or blender. Return to the saucepan over medium-low heat, add the cream, and heat just until hot—do not boil. Garnish with the popcorn and sliced basil.

SMOKY PUMPKIN BISQUE WITH SOY GLAZED SCALLOPS

This delicious, sophisticated soup submitted by Susan Asanovic took the grand prize in the 1997–98 Cookshack Smoked Foods Recipe Sweepstakes. Sea scallops can be substituted for the bay scallops; halve or quarter them if desired. Both the pumpkin and the scallops may be smoked up to a day ahead of time, then tightly covered and refrigerated.

MAKES 6 SERVINGS

SMOKY PUMPKIN BISQUE:
6 cups peeled, seeded, chopped pumpkin or butternut squash
2 teaspoons peanut oil
1 medium onion, chopped
1 teaspoon jerk seasoning blend
6 cups rich vegetable broth
1 cup unsweetened coconut milk
Salt to taste
SOY GLAZED SCALLOPS (recipe follows)
2 tablespoons toasted, unsalted pumpkin seeds, for garnish
1 bunch chopped cilantro, flat-leaf parsley, or marjoram leaves, for garnish

Place the pumpkin cubes on a mesh rack and set inside the smoker. Smoke for 1 hour at 190°F. Heat the peanut oil in a saucepan over medium heat. Add the onion and sauté until soft. Stir in the jerk seasoning. Add the smoked pumpkin and vegetable broth and bring to a boil. Reduce the heat and simmer, partially covered, for 15 minutes. Carefully purée the mixture in a blender or food processor. Return to the saucepan and add the coconut milk. Season to taste with salt and bring to a simmer over low heat. Serve the soup in heated soup bowls, and add some scallops in each bowl. Garnish with pumpkin seeds and herbs, and serve immediately.

Soy Glazed Scallops
2 teaspoons toasted sesame oil or roasted pumpkinseed oil
1 tablespoon reduced-sodium soy sauce
½ teaspoon sugar
Pinch of cayenne pepper
1⅓ pounds bay scallops

In a medium nonreactive glass or stainless steel bowl, combine the sesame or pumpkinseed oil with the soy sauce, sugar, and cayenne. Add the scallops and marinate for 20 minutes.
Prepare the smoker with apple wood to 190°F and add the scallops. Smoke for 30 minutes.

SWEET POTATO CANAPÉ WITH SPICED RUM PEAR SAUCE

1 large sweet potato, halved
1 cup (2 sticks) butter, plus melted butter
for brushing the sweet potato
1 teaspoon cinnamon
½ teaspoon vanilla
½ teaspoon allspice
½ teaspoon nutmeg
½ cup sugar
⅓ cup chicken broth
2 cups heavy cream
1 can prepared croissant dough
(from the dairy section of the supermarket)
1 very ripe pear
1 ounce spiced rum

Preheat the smoker to 225°F with 1 ounce of pecan or apple wood.
Brush the sweet potato with melted butter, place in a shallow pan, and smoke-cook until tender, about 2 hours. Remove the skin and cut the potato into cubes. Place in a medium saucepan and add 3 tablespoons butter, cinnamon, vanilla, allspice, nutmeg, 3 tablespoons sugar, and the chicken broth. Cook and stir for a few minutes to combine well.
Add 2 tablespoons heavy cream. Stir until creamy and smooth; the mixture should be somewhat firm. Pop the croissant can, unroll the croissant dough, and separate. Place a spoonful of the sweet potato mixture on each croissant and fold over to enclose the filling, pinching the end seams together. Brush the tops with melted butter and bake as directed on the label.
Peel and core the pear, reserving as much juice as possible. Cut into small pieces, place in a food processor, and purée. Reserve 1 tablespoon of sugar. In a small saucepan, combine the puréed pear with the remaining butter, remaining sugar, and spiced rum, stirring constantly on low heat until the sugar caramelizes. In a medium bowl, beat the heavy cream with the remaining

tablespoon of sugar to form stiff peaks. Place each stuffed croissant in a shallow bowl, drizzle liberally with the pear sauce, and top with a dollop of whipped cream.

APPLE-SMOKED TROUT AND AVOCADO QUICHE WITH SMOKED CHEDDAR

Serve this as a dinner-party appetizer. It's also great for breakfast or brunch.

1 premade 12-inch deep-dish pie crust
1 dozen eggs
½ teaspoon kosher salt
¼ teaspoon black pepper
¼ pound smoked trout filet, crumbled
¼ pound peeled and diced fresh avocado
1 teaspoon fresh lemon juice
1 tablespoon minced fresh chives
⅔ cup grated smoked cheddar cheese

Preheat the oven to 350°F. Blind-bake the pie crust just until lightly browned.
Set aside. In a large bowl, combine the eggs, salt, and pepper and mix well.
Stir in the smoked trout, avocado, lemon juice, chives, and half the grated cheddar.
Pour into the prebaked pie crust and top with the remaining smoked cheddar.
Bake for about 30 minutes, or until a knife inserted into the center can be removed without
liquid egg visible. Cool, cut into wedges, and serve.

SMOKED SALMON CHEESECAKE

People who have smokers often have smoked salmon on hand. Here's a savory way to use it.
Serve at room temperature with your favorite crackers or melba toast.

CRUST:
1 cup fine dry breadcrumbs
2 tablespoons melted butter
2 teaspoons dried dill

FILLING:
½ pound double-smoked bacon, finely chopped
4 to 5 green onions, chopped
3 (8-ounce) packages cream cheese, at room temperature
3 eggs
⅓ cup light cream
½ teaspoon salt
½ pound smoked salmon, coarsely chopped
1 cup grated Swiss cheese

Preheat the oven to 350°F. In a small bowl, combine the crumbs, butter, and dill.
Press into the bottom of a 9-inch springform pan. Bake for 6 to 8 minutes, or until golden.
Reduce the oven temperature to 300°F. In a large skillet over medium heat,
cook the bacon until crisp. Drain on paper towels. Add the green onions to the skillet and
sauté for 1 minute, then set aside to cool. In a large bowl, beat cream cheese, eggs, cream,
and salt until smooth. Stir in the salmon, grated cheese, bacon, and onions.
Pour the filling over the crust and bake for 75 minutes.
Turn off the oven, open the door slightly, and let the cheesecake cool in the oven for 1 hour.
When cool, cover and refrigerate for at least 2 hours before removing the sides of the pan.

SMOKED DEVILED EGGS

The key to boiling eggs successfully is using lots of water.
Plunging the cooked eggs into ice water makes them easier to peel.

6 eggs
½ teaspoon cumin
1 tablespoon finely chopped cilantro
3 tablespoons sweet pickle relish
½ teaspoon salt
Mayonnaise to taste
Black pepper to taste

Preheat the smoker to 225°F. Place the eggs in a large saucepan, cover with cold water,
bring to a full boil, cover, and turn off the heat. Let sit for 12 minutes.
When cool enough to handle, remove the shells. Place the peeled eggs in the smoker and smoke for
45 minutes. Halve the eggs lengthwise and use a teaspoon to remove the yolks.
In a small bowl, loosely combine the yolks with the cumin, cilantro, pickle relish, salt, and just
enough mayonnaise to bind the mixture. Divide the filling among the halved egg whites,
season with black pepper, cover, and refrigerate until ready to serve.

SMOKED RATTLESNAKE

1 large rattlesnake (2 to 3 pounds), skinned
2 tablespoons butter, melted
1 tablespoon granulated garlic
1 tablespoon granulated onion
½ tablespoon salt
½ tablespoon pepper
1 tablespoon Creole seasoning (optional)

Preheat the smoker to medium heat with hickory or oak wood.
Coil the snake and place it on a sheet of heavy foil. Fold up the edges of the foil to
form a shallow pan. Pour the melted butter over the snake.
Sprinkle with garlic, onion, salt, pepper, and Creole seasoning.
Place on a rack in the smoker and smoke for 1 to 2 hours, or until the meat flakes.

PORK

DAVE'S CAJUN BUTT

This recipe, developed by David Gross of Baton Rouge, Louisiana, was the Grand Prize winner in the 2000–2001 Cookshack Recipe Contest. Reduce the quantity of red pepper flakes if you prefer a less spicy dish.

6 pounds boneless pork butt
5 garlic cloves, cut into slivers
3 tablespoons dried red pepper flakes
¼ cup yellow mustard
3 tablespoons Cookshack Spicy Chicken Rub,
or your favorite Cajun seasoning
3 tablespoons brown sugar
1 teaspoon black pepper

Using a sharp knife, cut slits 1 inch deep all over the external surface of the pork. Using your thumb, press 1 garlic sliver and some red pepper flakes into each slit, then pinch the meat to close the slit. In a bowl, combine the mustard, chicken rub or Cajun seasoning, sugar, and black pepper. Mix well and apply to butt. Lightly dust with a coating of red pepper flakes. Wrap in plastic wrap and refrigerate overnight. Preheat the smoker with apple and hickory chips. Smoke-cook the pork butt for 1 hour per pound, or until the meat reaches an internal temperature of 190°F.

DELICIOUS CAROLINA BOSTON BUTT

This recipe from Lonnie Moore won second place for Traditional Pit Barbecue in Cookshack's 2000–2001 Recipe Contest. Serve the pulled pork with bread and pickles, and garnish with Bermuda onions, if desired.

4 to 6 pounds boneless Boston butt (pork butt)
1½ cups cider vinegar
3 tablespoons grated onion
5 tablespoons ketchup
1½ teaspoons salt
1½ teaspoons black pepper
1½ teaspoons hot sauce
2½ teaspoons Worcestershire sauce
½ teaspoon cayenne pepper
5 garlic cloves, minced
1½ cups brown sugar

Trim the fat from the pork butt. In a large zipper-lock plastic bag, combine the vinegar, onion, ketchup, salt, pepper, hot sauce, Worcestershire, cayenne, garlic, and sugar. Add the pork butt, seal the bag, and refrigerate for 12 to 24 hours, turning the bag occasionally. Preheat the smoker to 215°F to 220°F. Remove the pork butt from the bag, reserving the marinade in the refrigerator, and place in the smoker. Smoke-cook the pork for 14 hours. When cool enough to handle, shred the pork and cover with foil. In a small saucepan, bring the reserved marinade to a boil over medium heat and cook for 3 minutes. Serve the pulled pork with the marinade.

SMOKE-COOKED BOSTON BUTT

8 pounds boneless pork butt
Cookshack Rib Rub

Preheat the smoker to 225°F with 12 ounces of hickory wood.
Season the pork with the rub. Place in the smoker and smoke-cook for 12 hours.
To serve, pull the pork into small pieces and pile on soft buns for sandwiches.

COOKSHACK SPICED PORK BUTT

Here's a slightly spicier way to smoke-cook the flavorful pork butt, also known as Boston butt. Leaving the rub on overnight helps it permeate the meat.

5 pounds boneless pork butt
3 tablespoons Cookshack Rib Rub
Cookshack Spicy Barbecue Sauce

Season the pork with the rub. Cover and refrigerate for at least 8 hours.
Preheat the smoker to 225°F with 4 ounces of hickory wood. Place the pork in the smoker and smoke-cook for 10 hours. Serve with barbecue sauce.

SUGAR-RUBBED BOSTON BUTT

This recipe calls for a syringe specially designed to inject meats with a flavorful marinade before they're smoked. Every true barbecue aficionado owns one.

2 cups apple juice concentrate
3 cups brown sugar
1 teaspoon garlic powder
1 teaspoon cayenne pepper
8 pounds boneless pork butt

In a small bowl, combine the apple juice concentrate, 1 cup of the sugar, garlic powder, and cayenne. Transfer to a syringe, and inject the pork roasts with the marinade. Preheat the smoker to 250°F with 2 ounces of hickory wood. Place the pork in the smoker and smoke-cook for 8 hours. Remove the pork from the smoker, rub with the remaining 2 cups of the sugar, and wrap in foil. Return to the smoker and smoke-cook for 4 hours longer. Remove from the smoker and let rest for 30 minutes before pulling the meat into shreds. Serve on sandwich buns.

SMOKY SOW SANDWICH WITH BBQ SAUCE AND MARINATED COLESLAW

This recipe from Sherry Pate won best of category for Traditional Pit Barbecue in Cookshack's 2000–2001 Recipe Contest.

½ cup kosher salt
½ cup paprika
½ cup black pepper
2 tablespoons meat tenderizer
1 boneless pork roast (3 to 4 pounds), with fat left on
Smoky Sow BBQ Sauce (recipe follows)
Smoky Sow Sandwich Marinated Coleslaw (see page TK)
8 kaiser rolls

Preheat the smoker with pecan or oak wood to 175°F. Combine the salt, paprika, pepper, and meat tenderizer. Rub over the entire surface of the pork roast. Smoke-cook for at least 8 hours. When the pork is done, remove it from the pit and allow it to stand at room temperature for 15 to 20 minutes. Shred the pork into bite-sized pieces and reserve. Warm the kaiser rolls. Place about a cup of the shredded pork on the bottom half of each roll. Add a generous amount of the Smoky Sow Sandwich Marinated Coleslaw and top with 2 tablespoons of Smoky Sow BBQ Sauce. Top each sandwich with the remaining half of the roll and serve.

Smoky Sow BBQ Sauce
¼ pound (1 stick) butter
6 cloves garlic
1 onion, chopped
1 lemon, diced
¼ cup strong coffee
1 cup ketchup
1 cup Worcestershire sauce
½ cup cider vinegar
½ cup dark molasses
½ cup vegetable oil
1 tablespoon salt
1 tablespoon black pepper
1 tablespoon paprika
1 cup whiskey

In a medium saucepan, combine the butter, garlic, onion, lemon, coffee, ketchup, Worcestershire, vinegar, molasses, oil, salt, pepper, and paprika. Simmer over low heat for about 2 hours, or until the onions are tender and the sauce thickens. Remove from the heat and add the whiskey. Mix well and strain through a sieve or purée in a blender or food processor.

THYME-SMOKED PORK TENDERLOIN WITH SWEET ORANGE SAUCE

This recipe from Jon Sparrow won best of category for Wood-Smoked Foods in the Cookshack 2000–2001 Recipe Contest.

SERVES 4 TO 6

2 pork tenderloins (12 ounces each)
¾ cup fresh orange juice
3 tablespoons soy sauce
3 tablespoons Dijon mustard
2 tablespoons sugar
2 cloves garlic, crushed
½ teaspoon freshly ground black pepper
¼ cup chopped fresh thyme plus 1 sprig whole thyme

SAUCE:
3 tablespoons butter
½ cup fresh orange juice
¼ cup dry white wine
1 tablespoon soy sauce
½ cup orange marmalade
1 tablespoon Dijon mustard
4 orange slices
4 sprigs fresh thyme

Place the pork tenderloins in a large zipper-lock plastic bag.
Combine the orange juice, soy sauce, mustard, sugar, garlic, pepper, and
thyme. Pour over the pork tenderloins, seal the bag,
and refrigerate for 8 hours, turning occasionally. Preheat the smoker to 200°F.
Drain the pork and discard the marinade. Place the pork in the smoker. Add 2 ounces apple or
hickory wood and lay the sprig of thyme on top of the wood. Smoke-cook until the pork
reaches an internal temperature of 145°F. Let the pork rest for 15 minutes.

To make the sauce, melt the butter in a small saucepan over medium low heat.
Add the orange juice, wine, and soy sauce. Cook until slightly reduced.
Stir in the marmalade and mustard and cook until heated through.
To serve, cut the pork into thin slices. Drizzle with the sauce and garnish with
the orange slices and sprigs of fresh thyme.

STUFFED SMOKED PORK TENDERLOIN

½ pound shrimp, shelled and deveined
¼ cup (½ stick) butter
1 box seasoned stuffing mix for pork chops
2 pork tenderloins, 2 pounds each
2 tablespoons Cookshack Spicy Chicken Rub

Coarsely chop the shrimp. In a medium skillet, melt the butter.
Add the shrimp and sauté until just cooked through. Following the directions on the box,
prepare the stuffing mix. Combine the shrimp with the stuffing and allow to cool.
Remove any membrane and fat from tenderloins, and cut each one into pieces about
4 inches long. Carefully insert a boning knife through the center of each tenderloin piece, beginning
at a short end, and rotate the knife to form a hole through to the other short end.
Stuff each tenderloin piece with the stuffing mixture. Lightly dust the chicken rub.
Preheat the smoker to 225°F with 2 ounces of apple wood. Smoke-cook for 1½ hours.

SMOKED TASSO PORK LOIN

Morton's Tenderquick is a curing product that's available online from butcher-shop sites.

5 pounds boneless pork
2 ounces Morton's Tenderquick
½ ounce white pepper
¼ ounce black pepper
⅛ ounce cayenne pepper
½ ounce ground allspice
¼ ounce dried oregano
½ ounce paprika

Trim any fat and silverskin from the pork loin. Place the Tenderquick in a large bowl,
add the pork loin, and rub to coat well. Cover with plastic wrap and refrigerate for 5 to 6 hours.
Remove the loin, rinse well under cold water, and pat dry.
In a large bowl, combine the peppers, cayenne, allspice, oregano, and paprika.
Add the pork and rub to coat well, pressing the seasonings into the meat. Cover with plastic wrap
and refrigerate for 8 hours. Preheat the smoker to 200°F with 2 ounces of hickory wood.
Add the pork loin and smoke-cook for 2½ hours, until the meat reaches an internal temperature
of 155°F. To serve warm as a main course, cut into thick slices.
To serve cold in a sandwich, slice thinly.

SOUTHWEST SMOKED PORK TENDERLOIN WITH BARBECUE SAUCE

2 pounds pork tenderloin
4 tablespoons Southwest Seasoning (recipe follows)
1 cup Cookshack Spicy Barbecue Sauce
¼ pound (1 stick) butter

Remove any fat or silverskin from the tenderloin. Rub with 2 tablespoons of the Southwest Seasoning, cover, and refrigerate for at least 8 hours. Preheat the smoker to 225°F with 2 ounces of hickory wood. Place the pork in the smoker and smoke-cook for 1½ hours. To make the barbecue sauce, combine the remaining 2 tablespoons of Southwest Seasoning, barbecue sauce, and butter in a small saucepan, and cook, stirring occasionally, until the butter is melted.

SOUTHWEST SEASONING

MAKES ½ CUP

2 tablespoons chili powder
2 tablespoons paprika
1 tablespoon salt
1 tablespoon dried oregano
1 tablespoon ground coriander
1 tablespoon garlic powder
2 teaspoons ground cumin
1 teaspoon dried red pepper flakes
1 teaspoon cayenne pepper
1 teaspoon black pepper

In a medium bowl, combine the chili powder, paprika, salt, oregano, coriander, garlic powder, cumin, red pepper flakes, cayenne, and black pepper. Mix well.

PEPPER GARLIC PORK LOIN

½ pound bacon
1 large boneless pork loin roast (about 6 pounds), butterflied
2 jalapeño peppers, seeds and ribs removed, minced
¼ cup minced garlic
¼ cup barbecue sauce

Preheat the smoker to medium heat, using your favorite wood. Cover a work surface with plastic wrap and lay out the slices of bacon next to each other. Place the butterflied pork loin on top of the bacon slices. Combine the jalapeños, garlic, and barbecue sauce and spread over the inside of the pork. Carefully roll up the pork and bacon, and tie at intervals. Place the pork in the smoker and smoke-cook until the bacon is crisp. When sliced for serving, the pork should have a half-inch smoke ring.

PORK TENDERLOIN DELUXE

This pork is good whether served hot or cold. Try it thinly sliced in a sandwich with your favorite barbecue sauce or condiments.

2 pork tenderloins (about 1½ pounds each)
¼ cup honey
¼ cup soy sauce
¼ cup oyster sauce
2 tablespoons brown sugar
1¼ tablespoons finely chopped ginger
1 tablespoon minced garlic
1 tablespoon ketchup
¼ teaspoon onion powder
¼ teaspoon cayenne pepper
¼ teaspoon cinnamon

Place the tenderloins in a large nonreactive glass or stainless steel container. In a medium bowl, combine the honey, soy sauce, oyster sauce, sugar, ginger, garlic, ketchup, onion powder, cayenne, and cinnamon. Pour over the pork, cover, and refrigerate for 8 hours, turning occasionally. Preheat the smoker to 225°F. Remove the pork from the marinade and smoke for 2 to 3 hours, basting with reserved marinade if desired.

BOURBON AND HONEY SMOKE-ROASTED PORK TENDERLOIN

1 cup olive oil
¼ cup soy sauce
½ cup bourbon
½ cup thinly sliced onion
3 tablespoons honey
2 tablespoons fresh sage
½ cup lemon juice
1 tablespoon minced garlic
2 teaspoons black pepper
1½ tablespoons fresh ginger
1 teaspoon salt
3 pork tenderloins

In a large nonreactive glass or stainless steel container, combine the olive oil, soy sauce, bourbon, onion, honey, sage, lemon juice, garlic, pepper, ginger, and salt. Add the pork tenderloins and turn to coat with the marinade. Cover and refrigerate for 24 hours, turning occasionally. Preheat the grill. Remove the pork from the marinade and pat dry with paper towels. Roast for about 40 minutes. If the pork is to be served hot, allow it to sit on the edge of the grill for about 10 minutes after it is cooked, to allow the juices to settle.

PULLED PORK GREEN CHILE STEW

This recipe can also be made with 1 pound of browned and drained ground beef, but the smoked pulled pork, if you have some on hand, makes it special. The dish tastes even better the day after you prepare it.

1 tablespoon vegetable oil
1 medium onion
1 garlic clove, crushed
1 (14½-ounce) can beef broth
1 (8-ounce) can tomatoes
4 (14½-ounce) cans water
2 (3-ounce) packages pork gravy mix
1 (16-ounce) can refried beans
1 (8-ounce) can mild green chiles, chopped

1 (8-ounce) can hot green chiles, chopped
3 pounds baking potatoes, smoked, cooled, and diced
¾ pound smoked pulled pork
1 teaspoon garlic salt
1 teaspoon black pepper

In a large heavy pot, warm the oil over medium heat. Add the onion and garlic and sauté until translucent. Add the beef broth, tomatoes, water, gravy mix, beans, and green chiles.
Bring to a boil, then reduce heat to low and simmer for 20 to 30 minutes, stirring occasionally. Add the potatoes, pulled pork, garlic salt, and pepper and simmer for 10 minutes longer.
Cover, turn off the heat, and let stand for 10 minutes before serving.

BARBECUE SMOKED SPARE RIBS

3 to 4 pounds pork spare ribs
1 large onion, thinly sliced
1 lemon, thinly sliced
Dale's Steak Seasoning Sauce to taste
1 cup brown sugar
½ cup ketchup
¼ cup Worcestershire sauce
¼ cup cider vinegar
¼ cup chili sauce
⅓ cup soy sauce
2 teaspoons dry mustard
2 cloves garlic, chopped

Preheat the smoker. Cover the ribs with the onion rings and lemon slices, and place in the smoker. Smoke for 10 to 12 hours. In a medium saucepan, combine the steak sauce, sugar, ketchup, Worcestershire, vinegar, chili sauce, soy sauce, mustard, and garlic and bring to a boil. Baste the ribs with the sauce occasionally while smoking.

ST. LOUIS-STYLE RIBS

12 slabs St. Louis-style ribs (about 1¾ pounds each)
Cookshack Rib Rub
Cookshack Spicy Barbecue Sauce

Using a sharp knife, remove any membrane from the ribs. Season with the dry rub, wrap in foil, and refrigerate for 8 hours. Preheat the smoker to 225°F with 8 ounces of hickory wood. Place the ribs on rib racks, if available, and set in the smoker. Smoke-cook for 3½ hours. To serve, cut between the bones and serve with the barbecue sauce.

TORTUGA HONEYSUCKLE RIBS

Tortuga Citrus Honey is a commercial product from the Caribbean. Regular honey may be substituted. Serve these ribs with coleslaw, baked beans, and cornbread, and provide a large empty bowl for the bones, or "dead soldiers."

3 to 4 slabs baby back ribs
Dry rub of your choice
Fresh pineapple slices
2 teaspoons lemon juice
1 teaspoon lime juice
3 tablespoons cherry brandy
Hot and spicy barbecue sauce of your choice (preferably "Bone Suckin' Sauce")
¼ cup Tortuga Citrus Honey
1 to 2 teaspoons turbinado sugar (sold as "Sugar in the Raw")

One day before serving, prepare the ribs by peeling away the membrane and cutting away any excess fat. Apply a moderate amount of dry rub, cover with plastic wrap or foil, and refrigerate for at least 8 hours.
Place the pineapple in a nonreactive glass or stainless steel container.
Combine the lemon juice, lime juice, and cherry brandy, and pour over the pineapple.
Cover and refrigerate for at least 8 hours. Preheat the smoker to 225°F with apple wood.
Place the ribs in the smoker and smoke for 3½ hours. Increase the temperature to 250°F and smoke for 1 hour longer, basting with barbecue sauce during the last 20 minutes of smoking.
The internal temperature should read 170°F on a meat thermometer. Place the pineapple slices in the smoker 30 minutes before serving; reserve the marinade, and add the honey.
During the final 5 minutes of smoking, baste the ribs with the pineapple marinade mixture.
Place 3 pineapple slices on top of each slab of ribs, and lightly sprinkle with the sugar.
Allow the ribs to sit for 10 minutes before serving.

SMOKED BARBECUE RIBS

2 pounds home-style ribs
Salt and black pepper to taste
2 tablespoons brown sugar
2 tablespoons cumin
2 tablespoons chili powder
1 tablespoon cayenne pepper
¼ cup yellow mustard
Barbecue sauce of your choice

Bring a large pan of water to a boil, add the ribs, and boil for 7 to 10 minutes.
Drain and let cool. Preheat the smoker to 225°F. In a medium bowl, combine the salt, pepper, sugar,
cumin, chili powder, cayenne, and mustard. Rub the mixture over the ribs.
Place in the smoker and smoke-cook until lightly brown on each side, about 2 hours.
Preheat the grill. Make an 11-x-11-inch square pan by doubling a sheet of foil and folding it up
about 1 inch on the sides. Place the ribs in the foil and cover with barbecue sauce.
Place on the grill for about 20 minutes, until the sauce starts to caramelize.

BUBBA-Q RIBS

3½ pounds pork spareribs
Mustard
Garlic
Salt
Onion salt
Celery salt
Cumin
Chili powder
Melted butter
Corn syrup

Preheat the smoker with oak and pecan wood to 250°F.
Peel away any membrane from the ribs. Prepare a rub by combining the mustard, garlic,
salt, onion salt, celery salt, cumin, and chili powder to taste, and rub on the ribs. Smoke-
cook for 3 hours. Remove from the smoker, coat with a mixture of equal parts butter
and corn syrup, and wrap in foil. Smoke over apple wood at 250°F for 45 minutes.

CURED HICKORY-SMOKED BABY BACK RIBS

*Prague powder #1, a meat-curing product composed of salt, nitrate, and other ingredients,
is available from online butcher supply companies, as is powdered dextrose.*

1¼ gallons cold water
¾ cup pickling salt
1 cup powdered dextrose
3 tablespoons plus 1 teaspoon Prague powder #1
4 pounds pork spareribs

In a container large enough to hold the ribs, combine the water, pickling salt, dextrose, and
Prague powder. Mix well. Add the slabs of ribs to the cold brine. Refrigerate for 24 hours, stirring
and turning the ribs after 12 hours. Remove the ribs from the brine.
Set up an electric fan and place the ribs on a flat pan in front of the fan. Air-dry for 6 to 8 hours,
until the ribs are dry to the touch. Preheat the smoker with 2 ounces of hickory chunks to
225°F. Add the ribs and smoke-cook for 2 hours. Remove the ribs and let cool for 5 to 10 minutes
before serving. These ribs are just as good without a finishing sauce as they are with one!

COOKSHACK SMOKED BABY BACK RIBS

1½ pounds (3 slabs) baby back ribs
3 tablespoons Cookshack Rib Rub
3 tablespoons Cookshack Spicy Chicken Rub
Cookshack Spicy Barbecue Sauce

Prepare the ribs by peeling away the membrane and cutting away any excess fat.
Cut each slab in half. In a small bowl, combine the rib rub and chicken rub.
Rub the ribs well with the rub mixture. Cover and refrigerate for at least 8 hours.
Preheat the smoker to 225°F with 2 ounces of hickory wood. Place the ribs in the
smoker and smoke-cook for 3½ hours. To produce meat that's so tender it's falling off
the bone, wrap the ribs in foil at this point and cook for 45 minutes longer.
Serve with barbecue sauce.

BIG DADDY'S FAMOUS SMOKED BABY BACK RIBS

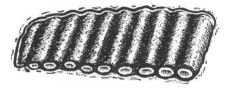

2 racks pork ribs
4 bottles Red Rock ginger ale
2 cups tomato sauce
1 cup Roddenberry's Cane Patch Syrup (or corn syrup)
¼ cup Worcestershire sauce
2 cloves garlic, chopped
¼ cup finely chopped onion
2 tablespoons ground ginger
1 teaspoon cayenne pepper
¼ cup water

Place the ribs in a large zipper-lock plastic bag.
Add the ginger ale, seal the bag, and refrigerate for at least 8 hours.
To make the sauce, combine the tomato sauce, syrup, Worcestershire sauce, garlic,
onion, ginger, cayenne, and water in a medium saucepan. Simmer over low heat
for 3 to 4 hours, adding water as needed to maintain a smooth consistency.
Preheat the smoker to 225°F with pre-moistened apple wood chips.
If your smoker requires liquid, use apple juice in place of water. After about 4 hours,
remove the ribs, coat with the sauce, and return to the smoker for 1 hour more.

HOWARD'S BABY BACK RIBS

5 pounds baby back ribs
Seasoned salt and black pepper
Dry rub of your choice (optional)
7 garlic cloves, finely chopped
2 jalapeños, finely chopped
2 red bell peppers, thinly sliced
2 green bell peppers, thinly sliced
2 yellow bell peppers, thinly sliced
2 onions, thinly sliced
Barbecue sauce of your choice

Season the ribs with salt, pepper, and dry rub if desired. Combine the garlic and jalapeños and rub on the ribs. Place the ribs in a nonreactive glass or stainless steel container and top with the sliced peppers and onions. Cover with foil and refrigerate for up to 48 hours. Remove the ribs from the refrigerator about an hour before smoking them. Preheat the smoker to 225°F. Set the ribs in the smoker and smoke for 10 to 12 hours. During the final hour, baste lightly with barbecue sauce.

SMOKED SAUSAGE

This recipe also works for bratwurst.
Serve the sausage and onions in French rolls with deli mustard.

1 tablespoon olive oil
5 garlic cloves, minced
1 white onion, thinly sliced
4 (12-ounce) bottles of your favorite beer
1 cup soy sauce
2 tablespoons brown sugar
1 tablespoon chili powder
Black pepper to taste
6 Italian sausages (recipe follows)

Preheat the smoker to 225°F. Warm the oil in a large sauté pan and add the garlic and onion. Sauté until softened. Add the beer, soy sauce, sugar, chili powder, and pepper and bring to a boil. Reduce the heat to low and add the sausages. Place in the smoker and smoke for 3 to 3½ hours. Remove the sausages and onions with a slotted spoon and serve.

ITALIAN SAUSAGE

This sausage is medium hot. If sausage casings are not available, form the meat mixture into patties and grill them instead of smoking.

SERVES 6

2 pounds coarsely ground pork butt
¼ cup plus 2 tablespoons red wine
1½ large garlic cloves, finely chopped
2 tablespoons ground aniseed
½ teaspoon cayenne pepper
½ teaspoon dried red pepper flakes
1½ teaspoons thyme
1½ teaspoons oregano
1½ teaspoons kosher salt
2 teaspoons ground black pepper
⅛ teaspoon allspice
½ teaspoon ground bay leaf
1½ teaspoons ground basil
½ teaspoon ground rosemary
1 tablespoon parsley
4 feet hog casings, 32mm. diameter (optional)

In a large nonreactive glass or stainless steel container, combine all the ingredients except the casings. Mix well, adding water if necessary to create a smooth consistency, and stuff into the casings. Tie and cut to form sausages.

SPICY SAUSAGE

If sausage casings are not available, this sausage may be formed into patties.
It's delicious served on rolls with peppers and onions, or with spaghetti.

MAKES 5 POUNDS

5 pounds lean ground pork butt
⅓ cup water
1 tablespoon freshly ground black pepper
1½ tablespoons cayenne pepper
2½ tablespoons paprika
2 tablespoons salt
½ teaspoon oregano
4 garlic cloves, minced
⅓ cup white vinegar
Sausage casings (optional)

In a large bowl, combine the pork, water, pepper, cayenne, paprika, salt, oregano, garlic,
and vinegar. Mix well and stuff into sausage casings, or form into patties.
Preheat the smoker to 225°F. If using sausage casings, hang the sausages in the smoker on hooks,
and smoke for about 2 hours, or until a meat thermometer reads 155° to 160°F.
If making patties, form into small cakes, place on a rack, and smoke-cook for about 2 hours.

MAPLE-GLAZED BAKED HAM

This makes a nice addition to any holiday table.

10 pounds fully cooked ham
Pure maple syrup
1 cup whole or halved pecans

Preheat the smoker to 225°F with 2 ounces of pecan, cherry, or hickory wood.
Place the ham in the smoker and smoke-cook for 2 hours. Remove the ham and
score the surface with a sharp knife to create a diamond pattern.
Pour maple syrup over the ham, making sure that the syrup penetrates the cuts.
Place whole or half pecans over the top of the ham. Reduce the smoker temperature to 180°F.
Return the ham to the smoker and smoke-cook for 1 hour.

APPLE-SMOKED PORK CHOPS
WITH APPLEJACK GLAZE

4 bone-in pork chops, 1½ inches thick
1 cup apple juice concentrate
1½ cups maple syrup
1½ cups honey
1 clove garlic, crushed
3 cinnamon sticks
¼ teaspoon ground cloves
¼ cup bourbon

Preheat the smoker to 225°F with 2 ounces of apple wood. Place the pork chops in the smoker
and smoke-cook for 1½ hours. To make the glaze, combine the maple syrup, honey,
garlic, cinnamon, cloves, and bourbon in a saucepan. Bring to a boil, reduce the heat to
low, and simmer until reduced by half, stirring often. Remove the cinnamon sticks.
Remove the pork chops from the smoker, brush with the glaze, and return to the smoker
for 30 minutes longer. The remaining glaze can be used as a sauce.

BARBEQUE SMOKED PORK SANDWICH

Serve this shredded pork on kaiser rolls for a delicious sandwich.

1 bone-in pork shoulder
4½ cups apple cider
⅓ cup salt
6 allspice berries
1 bay leaf
2 sprigs thyme
2 cups barbecue sauce of your choice
Kaiser rolls

Trim away the fat and silverskin from the pork shoulder. In a nonreactive glass or stainless steel container large enough to hold the pork, combine the cider, salt, allspice, bay leaf, and thyme. Add the pork, cover, and refrigerate for 1 hour. Preheat the smoker to 225°F with hickory wood chips. Drain pork, place in the smoker, and smoke until the meat is falling off the bone. Let the pork cool before shredding it. Add the sauce and serve.

APPLE-WOOD-SMOKED BACON, TROUT, AND POTATO HASH

This recipe from Kelly Daniels makes a nice brunch dish, especially when topped with poached eggs.

SERVES 10

1 pound apple wood-smoked bacon (cooked with drippings reserved for later use)
4 pounds red-skinned potatoes, skins on
½ pound red onions, chopped
Salt and pepper
2 cups heavy cream
1 pound smoked trout filet, flaked
½ cup chopped scallions
1 teaspoon hot sauce

In a large skillet, cook the bacon slices over medium heat until crisp.
Strain and reserve the bacon fat. Steam or roast the potatoes until they are tender but still firm.
Cool and cut into ¾-inch cubes. Place enough bacon fat in the skillet to coat the bottom.
Add the onions and sauté until light golden. Add the potatoes and stir to combine.
Season with salt and pepper. Add the heavy cream and toss again lightly. Over medium heat,
reduce the cream and potato mixture until it has thickened enough to coat the back of a spoon.
Stir in the flaked smoked trout, scallions, and hot sauce, and serve.

BARBECUE PASTE

*Use this paste as a flavorful rub for 3 to 4 pounds of pork spare ribs, venison,
or other meat, and smoke it for about 10 hours.*

MAKES 1 CUP

1 teaspoon dry mustard
2 tablespoons Dale's Steak Seasoning Sauce or
other steak sauce
1 teaspoon garlic powder
2 pinches dried red pepper flakes
1 tablespoon coarsely ground black pepper
¼ pound (1 stick) butter, melted
Beer or water

In a medium bowl, combine the mustard, steak sauce, garlic powder, red pepper
flakes, black pepper, and butter. Add just enough beer or water to create a paste.

BEEF, LAMB, & GAME

BEEF BRISKET

8 to 10 pounds packer trim beef brisket
Cookshack Spicy Barbecue Sauce

Preheat the smoker to 225°F with 4 ounces of hickory wood.
Place the untrimmed brisket on the center grill of the smoker.
If necessary, roll the small end of the meat under to make the brisket
a uniform thickness. Smoke-cook for 14 hours. Slice and serve with barbecue sauce.

BEER BRISKET

*This recipe is from Rob Streit, chef and partner of
the Loose Caboose in Harper, Kansas.*

3 teaspoons onion powder
1 tablespoon garlic powder
2 teaspoons salt
2 teaspoons black pepper
1 tablespoon thyme
3 tablespoons granulated sugar
3 tablespoons brown sugar
5 pounds beef brisket
12 ounces beer

In a small bowl, combine the onion powder, garlic powder, salt, pepper, thyme, and sugars.
Rub generously all over the brisket and place in a nonreactive glass or stainless steel container.
Drizzle the beer over the brisket. Cover and refrigerate for at least 10 hours.
Preheat the smoker to 225°F with mesquite or hickory wood. Transfer the brisket to the
smoker and smoke-cook for 10 hours. To serve, slice across the grain of the meat.

COOKSHACK FLAT BEEF BRISKET

2 to 3 pounds flat-end beef brisket
Cookshack Spicy Barbecue Sauce

Preheat the smoker to 225°F with 4 ounces of hickory wood. Place the brisket on the center grill of the smoker. Smoke-cook for 3 hours. Remove the brisket from the smoker and place on a large sheet of heavy-duty aluminum foil. Add barbecue sauce to taste. Securely wrap the brisket in the foil and replace in the smoker. Smoke-cook for 3 hours longer. Slice and serve, or chop the meat for delicious barbecue sandwiches.

SMOKE-COOKED BEEF BRISKET

5 to 10 pounds packer trim beef brisket
Head Country All Purpose Rub
Cookshack Mild Barbecue Sauce

Preheat the smoker to 225°F with 4 ounces each of cherry and hickory wood. Trim the fat from between the muscles of the brisket. Season with the rub. Place in the smoker and smoke-cook for 14 hours. Slice thinly across the grain and serve with the barbecue sauce.

SMOKED BEEF BRISKET WITH FINISHING SAUCE

*This recipe from Aaron Brooks was a grand prize winner
in Cookshack's 2000–2001 Recipe Contest.*

BRISKET AND MARINADE:
½ cup orange juice
½ cup Coca-Cola
1½ tablespoons freshly ground black pepper
1½ tablespoons celery salt
1½ tablespoons cinnamon
1½ tablespoons sea salt
1½ tablespoons garlic pepper or garlic powder
1½ tablespoons oregano
10 pounds beef brisket, packer trim

RUB:
1½ tablespoons freshly ground black pepper
1½ tablespoons celery salt
1 tablespoon chili powder
1½ tablespoons sea salt
1½ tablespoons garlic pepper or garlic powder
1½ tablespoons oregano

FINISHING SAUCE:
¼ cup brown sugar
⅛ cup honey
⅛ cup orange juice
⅛ cup ketchup

Combine the orange juice, Coca-Cola, pepper, celery salt, cinnamon, salt, garlic pepper, and oregano in a large nonreactive glass or stainless steel container. Add the brisket and cover with plastic wrap. Marinate in the refrigerator for at least 2 hours and up to 24 hours. Remove the brisket, discard the marinade, and let the meat come to room temperature.

In a small bowl, combine the pepper, celery salt, chili powder, salt, garlic pepper, and oregano. Apply this rub mixture all over the brisket. Preheat the smoker to 225°F using a combination of hickory and oak wood. Add the brisket and smoke-cook for 12 hours. Remove the brisket and reduce the smoker temperature to 150°F. Place the brisket on a large piece of heavy-duty foil.

In a small bowl, combine the sugar, honey, orange juice, and ketchup. Pour this finishing sauce over the brisket and wrap securely in the foil. Smoke for 1 hour. Remove the brisket from the smoker and open the foil to let the steam escape. Let rest for 20 minutes.
Slice thinly across the grain, and serve with the accumulated juices.

JACK DANIEL'S BRISKET

Serve this tender beef on open-faced buns.

1 large, lean brisket (about 6 pounds)
12 ounces Coca-Cola
½ cup Jack Daniel's Whiskey
1 cup barbecue sauce (preferably Head Country or Cookshack brand)

Place the brisket in a large nonreactive glass or stainless steel container.
Pour in the Coca-Cola and the whiskey, cover, and refrigerate for at least 8 hours.
Preheat the smoker to 225°F with 4 to 5 ounces of hickory wood.
Place the brisket in the smoker and smoke for 2½ to 3 hours. Preheat the oven to 200°F.
Wrap the brisket in foil, place in the oven, and cook for 8 to 9 hours.
When the brisket is cool enough to handle, pull or slice the meat.
Place it in a crockpot set to high and add the barbecue sauce. Cook for 1 to 2 hours.

T-RAY'S BRISKET

4 cups brown sugar
4 cups granulated sugar
3 cups salt
1 cup paprika
½ cup onion powder
½ cup black pepper
½ cup chili powder
½ cup cayenne pepper
¼ cup garlic powder
¼ cup celery seed
5 to 10 pounds beef brisket

In a medium bowl, combine sugars, salt, paprika, onion powder, pepper, chili powder,
cayenne, garlic powder, and celery seed. Rub liberally on the brisket.
Wrap in plastic wrap and refrigerate for at least 8 hours.
Preheat the smoker to 210°F to 230°F. Remove the brisket from the refrigerator 1 hour
before smoking. Set in the smoker and smoke for 2 hours. Wrap in foil and return to the
smoker for 4 to 10 hours (check after 5 hours), until the internal temperature reaches 210°F.
Remove from the smoker and let sit for 1 hour before slicing.

SPARKY'S SMOKED BRISKET

1 brisket, 5 to 7 pounds, preferably packer trim
5 tablespoons seasoned salt
2 tablespoons chili powder
6 tablespoons brown sugar
3 tablespoons black pepper
2 tablespoons cayenne pepper
2 tablespoons garlic salt
2 tablespoons onion salt
1 teaspoon paprika
Mustard to taste

Soak the brisket in water for a while to open up the pores of the meat. After soaking, pat dry with paper towels. In a small bowl, combine the seasoned salt, chili powder, sugar, pepper, cayenne, garlic salt, onion salt, and paprika. Rub liberally on the brisket, coating it thickly. Cover and refrigerate the brisket for at least 3 hours. Preheat the smoker to 250°F. Remove the brisket from the refrigerator 1 hour before smoking, and coat it liberally with mustard. Place the brisket, fat side down, in the smoker and smoke for 1½ hours. Turn it fat side up and smoke for 1½ hours longer. Preheat the oven to 300°F. Remove the brisket from the smoker and wrap in foil. Bake for 3 hours, fat side up. Remove from the oven and let sit for 1 hour, still wrapped in foil.

BARBECUED BEEF BRISKET

10 to 14 pounds beef brisket
4 medium onions, chopped
Seasoned salt, black pepper, and garlic salt to taste
1 gallon barbecue sauce of your choice
4-pound jar orange marmalade
2 cups soy sauce
½ cup spicy mustard
1 pound brown sugar
1 ounce Maggi seasoning

Season the brisket generously on both sides with the seasoned salt, pepper, and garlic salt. Cover and refrigerate for at least 8 hours. Preheat the smoker to 180°F to 200°F with hickory wood. Place the brisket in the smoker and smoke-cook for 3½ hours. Preheat the oven to 250°F. Place the brisket in a large pan, and cover with water and chopped onions. Cook for 3½ hours. Let the meat cool and trim away the excess fat. Reduce the heat to 225°F. In a large bowl, combine the barbecue sauce, marmalade, soy sauce, mustard, sugar, and seasoning. Brush the mixture on the brisket and cook for 1 hour longer, basting occasionally with the sauce.

UNCLE BEN'S BEEF BRISKET

Be sure to select a quality beef brisket with a good marbling of fat.
The recipe was submitted by Ben Hollesen.

8 to 10 pounds beef brisket
Jim Beam Garlic Creole Marinade
Jim Beam Bourbon
Garlic pepper seasoning

The night before smoking, inject the brisket with a 10-to-1 ratio of marinade
and bourbon. Rub the brisket with garlic pepper seasoning.
Place in a nonreactive glass or stainless steel container and refrigerate for at least 8 hours.
Preheat the smoker to180°F to 200°F with apple or hickory wood.
Place the brisket in the smoker and smoke for 11 hours.
If desired, crisp the exterior of the brisket by finishing it briefly on a hot grill.

CHOPPED BRISKET SANDWICH

Serve the chopped brisket on slices of white bread.

10 pounds packer-trim beef brisket
1 cup onion salt
1 cup finely chopped garlic
3 cups Cookshack Spicy Barbecue Sauce

Preheat the smoker to 225°F with 4 ounces of hickory wood.
Trim away the fat from the sides of the brisket, but do not remove the fat on the
flat surface. Rub liberally with onion salt and garlic. Set the brisket in the smoker and
smoke for 14 hours. Remove from the smoker and cool. Chop into 2-inch pieces and
combine it with the barbecue sauce in a saucepan over medium heat. Cook, stirring
occasionally, until the brisket falls apart.

SMOKE-COOKED BEEF ROUND

Beef top round (14 to 20 pounds), inside cut

Preheat the smoker to 250°F, without adding wood.
Place the beef in the smoker and smoke-cook for 12 hours. If smoking more than
one roast, smoke-cook the additional roasts for 30 minutes longer.

SMOKY SWEET BEEF KEBABS

2 tablespoons onion powder
¼ cup Worcestershire sauce
2 tablespoons oregano
¼ cup cooking oil
Salt and pepper to taste
1 teaspoon vinegar
1 teaspoon chopped chile peppers (optional)
3 pounds beef cubes
3 pounds mixed vegetables (such as bell peppers, onions, and
cherry tomatoes), cut into 2-inch pieces
Wooden skewers

In a nonreactive glass or stainless steel container, combine the onion powder, Worcestershire,
oregano, oil, salt, pepper, vinegar, and chile peppers. Add the beef cubes, cover, and
refrigerate for 8 hours. Preheat the smoker to medium heat with a combination of hickory, apple,
and peach wood. Soak the wooden skewers in water for 1 hour before using. Alternate the
beef and vegetables on the skewers. Place in the smoker and smoke for 1 to 2 hours.

ROSEMARY-SMOKED PRIME RIB

1 cup kosher salt
1 cup finely chopped garlic
2 tablespoons chopped fresh rosemary, plus 3 fresh sprigs
6 pounds beef prime rib

In a small bowl, combine the salt, garlic, and rosemary. Rub on the beef, wrap in plastic wrap, and refrigerate for at least 8 hours.

Preheat the smoker to 250°F with 3 fresh rosemary sprigs in the wood box. Unwrap the beef, set it in the smoker, and smoke-cook for 2 hours. Open the smoker and let it cool to about 140°F. Smoke the beef for 2 hours longer before slicing and serving.

APPLE WOOD-SMOKED PRIME RIB

This recipe is similar to the preceding one, but the technique is different, and the rosemary flavor will be much more subtle in this one.

6 pounds beef prime rib
Kosher salt
Chopped fresh rosemary
Garlic salt
Coarsely ground black pepper

Season the prime rib with salt, rosemary, garlic salt, and pepper. Preheat the smoker to 225°F with 2 ounces of apple wood. (For additional flavor and aroma, place a heaping tablespoon of minced fresh garlic on the wood.) Smoke-cook the beef for 1½ hours for medium-rare meat; increase the cooking time for medium and medium-well. Open the smoker door to let some heat escape, then turn the smoker down to 140°F and leave the meat inside for 3 hours longer.

BLACKENED PRIME RIB STEAK

This recipe was submitted by Kevin McPike.

5 pounds prime rib roast
3 cloves garlic, chopped
Butter
Cajun-spiced dry rub

Preheat the smoker to 225°F. Rub the prime rib with the dry rub and garlic and place in the smoker. Smoke for 20 minutes per pound, until a meat thermometer registers 115°F. During the last 20 minutes of smoking, preheat the grill and heat a cast-iron skillet over the coals. Let the roast cool for 15 minutes, then cut into steaks 1 inch thick.
Melt the butter and Cajun seasoning in another skillet on the stovetop, and dip each steak into the mixture, coating it with butter on both sides. Place the steaks in the hot cast-iron skillet for 30 seconds per side, then remove to a serving plate.

BEEF LINKS

*This recipe came with a note that the sausages should be
"sliced and served with sauce and cheap white bread."*

4 pounds ground beef
1 cup water
1 tablespoon dried red pepper flakes
1 tablespoon paprika
2 tablespoons salt
2 tablespoons black pepper
1 teaspoon garlic powder
1 teaspoon onion powder
3 long sausage casings

In a large nonreactive glass or stainless steel container, combine the beef, water, red pepper flakes, paprika, salt, pepper, garlic powder, and onion powder. Mix well and transfer to zipper-lock plastic bags. Refrigerate for at least 8 hours. Preheat the smoker to 225°F with hickory chips. Stuff the sausage casings with the beef mixture. Place in the smoker and smoke for 1 hour.

SUMMER SAUSAGE

The Hi Mountain Seasonings Summer Sausage Kit called for in this recipe, which includes sausage casings, can be purchased from Hi Mountain Jerky, Inc. in Riverton, Wyoming, by calling 800-829-2285.

1 Hi Mountain Seasonings Summer Sausage Kit
6 pounds extra-lean ground beef or venison
3 pounds ground pork

Follow the directions in the sausage kit for seasoning and marinating the meat.
Stuff the seasoned meat into the sausage casings, cover, and refrigerate for
8 hours. Preheat the smoker to 140°F with 4 ounces of hickory wood.
Hang the sausages in the smoker from the top grill. Smoke-cook for 1 hour, then
increase the smoker temperature to 180°F for 2 hours.

PULLED BEEF BONES

*Start this recipe the day before you plan to eat it. Both oxtails and beef ribs
have a rich, distinctive flavor, with meat that becomes "falling-off-the-bone"
tender, but not mushy. Smoking produces a flavorful crust, known by
smoking fans as "bark." Serve it piled high on soft,
white buns, with coleslaw on the side.*

1 tablespoon plus 1 teaspoon celery salt
1 tablespoon salt
1½ teaspoons sugar
1½ teaspoons pepper
½ teaspoon onion powder
½ teaspoon garlic powder
2 oxtails, separated at the joints
6 meaty beef back ribs, about 4 inches long
1 (10½-ounce) can condensed beef broth
Tomato-based barbecue sauce of your choice

In a small bowl, combine the celery salt, salt, sugar, pepper, onion powder, and garlic powder.
Pour into a small paper bag and add the meat pieces a few at a time.
Shake well to cover with the rub, then transfer to a zipper-lock plastic bag and refrigerate.
Preheat the smoker to 230°F with oak or hickory wood. Place the oxtails and ribs in the
smoker and smoke for 3 hours, basting occasionally with the undiluted beef broth.
Wrap the meat in foil, baste with the broth, and seal tightly. Return to the smoker and smoke for
4½ hours longer. Unwrap the meat and return to the smoker for 30 minutes more.
Remove the meat from the bones and pull into shreds with a fork. Toss the shreds to combine
and add barbecue sauce to taste.

MEAT LOAF

2 pounds lean ground beef
2 eggs
1½ cups oats
⅔ cup salsa

Preheat the smoker to 225°F with 1 ounce of hickory wood. In a large bowl, combine the ground
beef, eggs, oats, and salsa. Place in a loaf pan and set in the smoker. Smoke-cook for 2 hours.

HAWAIIAN TRI-TIP

2 cups sea salt
2 cups crushed pineapple
2 cups minced garlic
1 cup brown sugar
2 to 2½ pounds beef tri-tip roast

In a large nonreactive glass or stainless steel container, combine the salt, pineapple, garlic, and sugar. Rub the beef with the seasoning mix, cover, and refrigerate for at least 8 hours. Preheat the smoker to 225°F with 2 ounces of cherry wood and 1 garlic clove. Place the beef in the smoker and smoke-cook for 2 hours. Slice thinly to serve.

SMOKED TRI-TIP

3 pounds beef tri-tip, trimmed
½ teaspoon garlic powder
½ teaspoon onion powder
1 tablespoon chili powder
¼ teaspoon cayenne pepper
1 teaspoon paprika
1 tablespoon brown sugar
½ teaspoon cumin
1 tablespoon salt
2 tablespoons sesame oil
3 tablespoons soy sauce

Trim most of the fat from the meat. In a mixing bowl, combine the garlic powder, onion powder, chili powder, cayenne, paprika, sugar, cumin, salt, sesame oil, and soy sauce, and mix to form a paste. Rub the mixture all over the beef, pressing it into the meat. Cover with plastic wrap and refrigerate for 8 hours.
Preheat the smoker to 275°F with 2 ounces of black walnut or hickory wood. Unwrap the meat and place it on a rack in the smoker. Smoke-cook for about 45 minutes, or until the meat reaches an internal temperature of 130°F for rare and 135°F for medium.
Let sit for 10 minutes and thinly slice against the grain to serve.

COUNTRY-SMOKED TENNESSEE TRI-TIP WITH TANGY SAUCE

2 tablespoons packed brown sugar
1 teaspoon paprika
½ teaspoon cumin
½ teaspoon cayenne pepper
2 teaspoons chili powder
1 teaspoon garlic salt
1 teaspoon onion salt
3 pounds beef tri-tip
3 tablespoons olive oil
Tangy Sauce (recipe follows)

In a small bowl, combine the sugar, paprika, cumin, cayenne, chili powder, garlic salt, and onion salt. Coat the tri-tip with the olive oil. Set aside ½ a tablespoon of the seasoning mixture, and rub the remainder into the beef. Preheat the smoker to 225°F with 2 ounces of hickory wood. Place the beef in the smoker and smoke-cook for 2 hours. Open the smoker door to reduce the heat, turn the smoker temperature down to 140°F, and leave the beef inside for 3 hours. After removing the beef from the smoker, glaze with Tangy Sauce and serve.

Tangy Sauce
¼ cup apple jelly
¼ cup ketchup
2 teaspoons cider vinegar
½ tablespoon reserved seasoning mixture (from above)

In a microwavable bowl, combine the jelly, ketchup, vinegar, and reserved seasoning mixture. Microwave at high power for 2 to 3 minutes, stirring occasionally, until the jelly is melted.

BEEF STRIP LOIN

⅓ cup Cookshack Spicy Chicken Rub
6 pounds beef strip loin (choice cut)

Preheat the smoker to 250°F with 2 ounces of hickory wood.
Generously rub the chicken spice on the beef loin. Place the beef in the smoker
and smoke-cook for 2 hours. Let cool for 30 minutes, then slice and serve.

SMOKED TENDERLOIN OF BEEF

1 whole beef tenderloin (8 pounds)
2 tablespoons minced garlic
2 tablespoons coarsely ground black pepper

Preheat the smoker to 140°F with 2 ounces of apple wood.
Rub the tenderloin with the garlic and pepper. Place in the smoker and smoke-cook
for 2 hours. Reduce the smoker temperature to 140°F and smoke-cook for
2 hours longer. Slice and serve.

MONTREAL STEAK

4 rib-eye or New York strip steaks, at least 1¼-inches thick
Montreal seasoning, or other spice blend of your choice

Coat the steaks with the Montreal seasoning or another spice blend. Preheat the smoker to 225°F
with 2 ounces of cherry wood. Place the steaks in the smoker and smoke-cook for about
55 minutes, or until the meat reaches an internal temperature of 140°F.

BEEF BACK RIBS

2 slabs (3 pounds each) beef back ribs
Cookshack Rib Rub
Cookshack Spicy Barbecue Sauce

Clean and remove any excess membrane, skin, and fat from the ribs.
Rub the ribs with rib rub, cover, and refrigerate for 8 hours.
Preheat the smoker to 225°F with 2 ounces of hickory wood. Place the ribs in
the smoker; if necessary, cut the slabs in half so they fit easily into the smoker.
Smoke-cook for 5 hours. Serve with barbecue sauce on the side.

STUFFED SMOKED FLANK STEAK

STEAK:
1½ pounds flank steak, trimmed
¼ cup olive oil
2 tablespoons lemon juice
2 cloves garlic, minced
1 tablespoon dried oregano
2 tablespoons minced red peppers
½ teaspoon sugar
¼ teaspoon salt

STUFFING:
2 tablespoons olive oil
¼ cup finely chopped onion
¼ cup finely chopped celery
2 cloves garlic, minced
½ pound andouille sausage, finely chopped
2 slices bread, finely chopped
1 egg
1 tablespoon chili powder
1 tablespoon cumin
Salt and pepper to taste

Slice the flank steak horizontally without cutting it into two pieces, and lay it out flat like an open book. In a large nonreactive glass or stainless steel bowl, combine the oil, lemon juice, garlic, oregano, red peppers, sugar, and salt. Mix well, add the flank steak, cover, and marinate for 2 to 3 hours.

To make the stuffing, heat the oil in a sauté pan. Add the onion, celery, garlic, and sausage, and sauté for 5 minutes. Remove from heat and add the bread, egg, chili powder, cumin, salt, and pepper. Place the stuffing in the center of the flank steak, roll up the meat, and tie in several places to secure. Preheat the smoker to 300°F with 2 ounces of mesquite wood. Place the meat in the smoker and smoke-cook, basting occasionally, for about 3 hours, or until the beef reaches an internal temperature of 150°F. Let rest for 10 minutes, remove the string, and slice against the grain to serve.

SMOKE-COOKED LEGS OF LAMB

Here's a simple recipe that feeds a crowd. It can be halved or quartered as desired.

4 bone-in legs of lamb (about 6 pounds each)

Preheat the smoker to 250°F with 3 sprigs of fresh rosemary in the wood box. Place one leg of lamb in the smoker and smoke-cook for 15 minutes per pound. Remove from the smoker and cook each additional leg for 15 minutes per pound, plus an extra 30 minutes.

HICKORY-SMOKED LEG OF LAMB

1 bone-in leg of lamb (about 6 pounds)
Salt

Preheat the smoker to 225°F with 4 ounces of hickory wood. Remove all sinew, fat, and membrane from the lamb. Sprinkle it lightly with salt. Place the lamb in the smoker and smoke-cook for 6 hours.

SMOKED BONELESS LEG OF LAMB

4 pounds boneless, butterflied leg of lamb, trimmed
½ cup chopped cilantro
2 stalks lemongrass, chopped
4 cloves garlic, chopped
3 tablespoons soy sauce
Juice of 1 lime, plus minced zest
1 teaspoon sugar
3 tablespoons olive oil

Spread the butterflied lamb open, like a book. In a small bowl, combine the cilantro, lemongrass, garlic, soy sauce, lime juice and zest, sugar, and olive oil. Rub the mixture over the lamb. Cover with plastic wrap and refrigerate for 8 hours.
Preheat the smoker to 275°F with 2 ounces of hickory wood. Place the lamb on a rack in the smoker, fat side up, and smoke-cook for 1½ hours, or until it reaches an internal temperature of 140°F. Let the lamb rest for 10 minutes before slicing.

OLIVE-CURED SMOKED LEG OF LAMB

1 head garlic
¼ to ½ cup olive oil
1 cup Kalamata olives, rinsed, drained, pitted, and pureed
Zest of 2 lemons
Chopped fresh thyme and rosemary to taste
4 pounds boneless, butterflied leg of lamb

Preheat a conventional oven to 350°F. Remove excess skin from the head of garlic. Moisten it with olive oil and wrap it in foil. Roast in the oven for 45 minutes. Cool and cut off about a ½-inch of the root section. Squeeze the roasted garlic out of the bulb. In a small bowl, combine the roasted garlic, olive puree, lemon zest, and enough olive oil to create a smooth paste. Add thyme and rosemary to taste. Spread the butterflied lamb open, like a book. Spread the olive paste on both sides of the lamb. Roll the lamb up, tie it with kitchen string, cover, and refrigerate for 8 hours, or for up to 2 days. Preheat the smoker to 250°F with 6 sprigs of fresh rosemary in the wood box. Smoke-cook for 2½ hours.

VENISON HAM

6 pounds venison ham or
other similar cut of venison
Vegetable oil
Garlic powder
Onion powder
Salt and pepper
Ground coriander
Ground celery powder
Bacon

Rub the venison with vegetable oil. In a small bowl, combine the garlic powder,
onion powder, salt, pepper, coriander, and celery powder to taste.
Rub the seasoning mixture on the venison. Cover the meat completely with bacon
strips, securing the bacon with toothpicks.
Cover with plastic wrap and refrigerate for 8 hours.
Preheat the smoker to 225°F with 2 ounces of hickory wood. Remove the plastic
from the venison and place it in the smoker. Smoke-cook for 6 hours. Remove the
bacon and toothpicks before serving.

VENISON JERKY

*If you make a lot of jerky, you may want to purchase special jerky rods, which
allow you to hang the meat vertically inside the smoker.*

1 pound venison
2 cups water
1 (12-ounce) can of beer
½ cup dry red wine
½ cup soy sauce
½ teaspoon garlic powder
½ teaspoon onion powder
2 teaspoons curing salt
2 teaspoons brown sugar
½ teaspoon dried red pepper flakes
¼ teaspoon ground mustard powder
½ teaspoon black pepper
1 tablespoon Worcestershire sauce

Using a very sharp knife, thinly slice the venison, with the grain of the meat.
The slices should be 6 to 8 inches long and 1 inch wide.
In a nonreactive glass or stainless steel container, combine the water, beer, wine, soy sauce, garlic powder, onion powder, salt, sugar, red pepper flakes, mustard powder, pepper, and Worcestershire.
Add the venison strips, cover, and refrigerate for at least 8 hours.
Preheat the smoker to 200°F with 2 ounces of hickory wood.
Remove the venison from the marinade and place it on seafood grills, if available.
Place in the smoker and smoke-cook for 2 hours, turning the meat and
rotating the grills after 1 hour.

CAJUN-STYLE JERKY

The Hi Mountain Jerky seasonings called for in this recipe can be purchased from
Hi Mountain Jerky, Inc. in Riverton, Wyoming, by calling 800-829-2285.

7 pounds inside round cut of venison or beef
1 Hi Mountain Seasonings Cajun Style Jerky Kit

Using a very sharp knife, thinly slice the venison or beef, with the grain of the meat.
The slices should be 6 to 8 inches long and 1 inch wide. Follow the directions in the jerky
kit for seasoning and marinating the meat. Preheat the smoker to 200°F with 2 ounces
of hickory wood. Remove the venison or beef from the marinade and place it on seafood grills,
if available. Place in the smoker and smoke-cook for 2 hours, turning the meat and
rotating the grills after 1 hour.

POULTRY & GAME BIRDS

JACK BLACK BBQ CHICKEN

In this recipe from Kelly Tomkins, the chicken is smoked and then roasted at a low temperature until the meat is literally falling off the bone.

2 chickens, cut into quarters
Cookshack Spicy Chicken Rub
Kraft Hickory Smoke Barbecue Sauce
Jack Daniels Black Label Tennessee Sour Mash Whiskey

Preheat the smoker to 225°F with 4 ounces of hickory wood.
Rinse and dry the chicken quarters and sprinkle both sides with the chicken rub.
Place in the smoker and smoke for 1 hour. Preheat the oven to 250°F.
Transfer the chicken pieces to a large roasting pan with a raised wire rack in the
bottom. (The rack should be about ¾ of an inch from the bottom.) Cover the pan with foil
and bake the chicken for 2 hours. Combine the barbecue sauce with the whiskey
at a ratio of 1 cup barbecue sauce to 2 tablespoons whiskey. Remove the chicken from
the oven, remove the skin, and brush liberally with the barbecue sauce mixture.
Serve with extra sauce on the side.

ORIENTAL SMOKED CHICKEN

This recipe is from Greg Fontenot.

1 chicken, halved lengthwise, with the backbone removed
1 orange, halved
2 tablespoons coarse salt
1 teaspoon black peppercorns
2 tablespoons loose black tea leaves
¼ cup brown sugar
½ cup rice
1 cup soaked oak chips

Place the chicken, cut side down, in a shallow bowl and squeeze the orange juice over it.
Add the orange halves to the bowl with the chicken. Place the bowl in a bamboo steamer and steam
over simmering water for 20 to 30 minutes. Preheat the grill. In a heatproof pan, combine the salt,
peppercorns, tea, sugar, rice, and oak chips. Place the pan over the fire of a grill and when it begins to
smoke, add the chicken, skin side down, on the grill grate over the smoke pan. Cover with foil and
smoke for 20 to 30 minutes, until the skin is golden brown.

"TARRED AND FIERY" CHICKEN

*Depending on your tolerance for spicy food, remove the seeds
from the jalapeños or leave them in.*

DRY RUB AND CHICKEN:
2 tablespoons coarsely ground black pepper
2 teaspoons ground thyme
1 teaspoon ground ginger
2 teaspoons onion powder
1 teaspoon garlic powder
3 pounds chicken parts

SAUCE:
1 cup cider vinegar
1 cup dark molasses
2 tablespoons brown sugar
1 cup minced onions
½ cup finely chopped green pepper
6 jalapeños, finely chopped
2 teaspoons salt
2 garlic cloves, finely chopped

In a small bowl, combine the pepper, thyme, ginger, onion powder, and garlic powder.
Rub the dry mixture liberally on the chicken. Cover and refrigerate for 2 to 3 hours.
Preheat the smoker for water-smoking with hickory to 160°F.
Smoke the chicken for 2 hours. Preheat the grill to medium high.
In a medium bowl, combine the vinegar, molasses, sugar, onions, green pepper,
jalapeños, salt, and garlic. Brush on the chicken and grill until fully cooked,
basting occasionally with the sauce.

TANDOORI SMOKED CHICKEN

1½ tablespoons salt
4 cloves garlic, minced
Juice of 1 lemon
3 chickens, halved, with backbones removed
1 cup plain yogurt
2 tablespoons Madras curry powder

In a small bowl, combine the salt, garlic, and lemon juice.
Rub the mixture all over the chickens. In another bowl, combine the yogurt and
curry powder. Coat each piece of chicken with the yogurt mixture, cover, and refrigerate for 8 hours.
Preheat the smoker to 250°F with 2 ounces of apple wood. Place the chicken on the smoker rack and
smoke-cook for 2 hours, until the chicken reaches an internal temperature of 170°F.

WORCESTERSHIRE WINGS

*Morton's Tenderquick is a curing product that's available
from online butcher-shop sites.*

¾ cup sugar cure Morton's Tenderquick
½ cup brown sugar, plus additional for rubbing
3 cups apple cider
¼ teaspoon ginger
2 tablespoons black pepper
¼ cup lemon juice
¼ ounce maple flavoring
2 quarts water
5 pounds chicken wings, cut in sections
2 tablespoons cayenne pepper (optional)
1 cup Worcestershire sauce

In a large nonreactive stainless steel pot, combine the sugar cure, brown sugar,
cider, ginger, pepper, lemon juice, maple flavoring, and water. Bring to a boil,
add the chicken wings, and simmer for 10 minutes. Remove the wings, drain,
and air-dry for 1 hour. Preheat the smoker to 225°F. Rub the wings with additional brown sugar
and sprinkle with cayenne if desired. Place in the smoker and smoke for 2 to 4 hours,
brushing occasionally with Worcestershire sauce.

SMOKED HOT WINGS

1 cup lemon juice
1 cup vegetable oil
2 tablespoons Louisiana Hot Sauce
2 tablespoons Tabasco
2 tablespoons chili powder
¼ cup brown sugar
24 chicken wings
Ranch salad dressing

In a large nonreactive glass or stainless steel bowl, combine the lemon juice,
vegetable oil, hot sauce, Tabasco, chili powder, and sugar.
Add the chicken wings, toss to coat well, cover, and refrigerate for at least 8 hours.
Preheat the smoker to 225°F with 4 ounces of hickory wood.
Drain the wings, place in the smoker, and smoke-cook for 1½ hours.
Serve with ranch dressing.

SMOKED CHICKEN BREAST WITH PAPAYA KIWI SALSA

4 boneless, skinless chicken breasts
4 flour tortillas, grilled
Papaya Kiwi Salsa (recipe follows)
4 cilantro sprigs, for garnish

Preheat the smoker to 225°F with 2 ounces of apple wood.
Place the chicken breasts in the smoker and smoke-cook for 1¼ hours.
Slice the breasts, keeping the slices together.
To serve, place a grilled tortilla on each serving plate.
Fan out one of the smoked chicken breasts on the tortilla, and top with Papaya
Kiwi Salsa. Garnish with a sprig of cilantro.

Papaya Kiwi Salsa
1 papaya, cut into rough chunks
3 kiwi fruit, cut into rough chunks
1 green bell pepper, seeds and ribs removed
1 red bell pepper, seeds and ribs removed
1 jalapeño pepper, seeds and ribs removed
1 cup sugar
Juice of 1 lime
Juice of 1 lemon

In a food processor, combine the papaya, kiwi, peppers, sugar, lime juice,
and lemon juice. Puree until almost smooth.

SMOKE-GLAZED CHICKEN BREASTS WITH SZECHUAN PEANUT DIPPING SAUCE

½ cup dark brown sugar
2 tablespoons paprika
1 teaspoon granulated garlic
¼ cup cornstarch
4 bone-in, skin-on chicken breasts
Szechuan Peanut Dipping Sauce (recipe follows)

In a small bowl, combine the sugar, paprika, garlic, and cornstarch. Rub the mixture on both
sides of the chicken breasts. Cover and refrigerate for at least 8 hours.
Preheat the smoker to 200°F. Make an open pouch of foil that will fit in the wood
box of the smoker and fill it with ¼ cup brown sugar, ¼ cup raw brown rice, and
¼ cup black tea leaves. Place the chicken breasts in the smoker and smoke-cook for 1 hour.
Preheat the gas or charcoal grill and grill the chicken breasts until fully cooked.
Serve with Szechuan Peanut Dipping Sauce on the side.

Szechuan Peanut Dipping Sauce

¼ cup water
2 tablespoons vegetable oil
⅓ cup white vinegar
⅓ cup soy sauce
1 tablespoon fresh lime juice
½ cup finely chopped onions
1 chicken bouillon cube
1 tablespoon granulated garlic
½ teaspoon ground ginger
½ teaspoon ground coriander
1 teaspoon cayenne pepper
¼ teaspoon nutmeg
1 teaspoon dried red pepper flakes
1 cup chunky natural peanut butter
½ cup honey

In a large saucepan, combine the water, oil, vinegar, soy sauce, lime juice, onions, bouillon cube, garlic, ginger, coriander, cayenne, nutmeg, and red pepper flakes. Cook over medium heat for 5 minutes, stirring frequently. Remove from the heat and stir in the peanut butter and honey. Mix well and serve.

SOUTHWEST STUFFED SMOKED CHICKEN BREAST

1 green bell pepper
1 yellow bell pepper
1 red bell pepper
3 jalapeño peppers
½ cup grated pepper jack cheese
4 boneless, skinless chicken breasts
Southwest Seasoning (see page TK)

Preheat a gas or charcoal grill. Place the peppers on the grill and roast until the skins are blackened. Wrap the peppers in foil or place in a paper bag. When the peppers have cooled enough to handle, peel away the charred skin. Remove the seeds and ribs and cut the peppers into narrow strips. Combine with the grated cheese and divide into four equal portions. Stuff each chicken breast with the pepper and cheese mixture, and wrap with kitchen string to secure the stuffing. Season the chicken with Southwest Seasoning. Preheat the smoker to 225°F with 2 ounces of hickory wood. Place the stuffed chicken in the smoker and smoke-cook for 1¼ hours. Remove the string from the chicken before serving.

SMOKED CHICKEN

This is a picnic standard with a smoky twist. If you have a vertical chicken roasting rack, use it here.

1 chicken (3 to 4 pounds)
Freshly squeezed lemon juice
Lemon pepper
Seasoned salt
Cookshack Spicy Barbecue Sauce

Preheat the smoker to 250°F with 4 ounces of mesquite. Rub the chicken inside and outside with lemon juice. Rub liberally with lemon pepper and seasoned salt, making sure to rub under the wings and legs. Place on the lower rack of the smoker and smoke for 4 hours. The chicken is done when a wing or leg can be easily pulled off. Brush lightly with barbecue sauce before serving.

SMOKED CHICKEN SALAD

This makes a great summer dish, served with your favorite bread or with crackers.

2 whole chicken breasts
Freshly ground black pepper
Seasoned salt
3 tablespoons mayonnaise
2 hard-boiled eggs, whites only
2 slices white onion
2 tablespoons pickle relish

Preheat the smoker to 220°F with apple wood. Coat the chicken breasts with pepper and seasoned salt, place in the smoker, and smoke for 2 to 2½ hours. Let the chicken cool, discard skin and bones, and tear into pieces. Place the chicken in the bowl of a food processor and chop. Add the mayonnaise, hard-boiled egg whites, onion, and pickle relish and process to chop well.

SMOKED CAPON WITH WILD RICE

Feel free to substitute hickory, mesquite, or pecan wood.

SERVES 6

1 large capon (6 pounds), rinsed thoroughly
¼ cup Cookshack Spicy Chicken Rub
2 tablespoons butter
4 cups water
2 cups long grain wild rice

Preheat the smoker to 210°F with 15 pounds of apple wood for water smoking.
Rub the capon, inside and outside, with the chicken rub. Place the capon in the
smoker and smoke for 30 to 45 minutes per pound of meat. Do not allow the temperature
to drop below 180°F. In a large saucepan, melt the butter over medium heat.
Add the rice, stir to coat with the butter, and cook for a few minutes.
Add 4 cups of water and bring to a boil. Boil for 5 minutes, then reduce the heat to low,
cover and simmer until the rice is done to your taste.
To serve, carve the capon and serve over the rice.

EASY AS PAELLA

Serve this with green salad and crusty bread.

1 chicken, cut into pieces
Salt and pepper to taste
¼ cup olive oil
2 cups rice
1 pound clams
1 pound smoked sausage, sliced into 1-inch pieces
2 cups chicken stock
1 cup chunky salsa
½ cup white wine
1 pound raw, peeled shrimp
1 cup frozen peas
Hot pepper sauce

Rinse the chicken pieces and pat dry with paper towels. Season with salt and pepper. In a large sauté pan, warm the olive oil over medium heat. Add the chicken and sauté until golden. Remove the chicken, add the rice, and sauté for 5 minutes. Add the chicken, clams, sausage, chicken stock, salsa, and wine. Cover, reduce the heat to low, and simmer for 20 minutes. Add the shrimp and frozen peas, cover, and continue cooking for 10 minutes longer. Season to taste with hot pepper sauce.

BRUNSWICK STEW FROM ALABAMA

1 large smoked chicken (about 5 pounds) or
2 small frying chickens (2½ pounds each), smoked
Vegetable oil
2 large onions, chopped
2 bell peppers, chopped
3 pounds heavily smoked pork (1 pound should be outside meat
with some browned pieces)
Chicken broth
1 (6-ounce) can tomato sauce
1 (6-ounce) bottle Worcestershire sauce
1 (1-gallon) can corn, drained
1 (1-gallon) can crushed tomatoes
2 (1-gallon) cans baby lima beans, drained
Salt and pepper
Hot sauce
Dried hot peppers

Remove the skin and bones from the chicken and tear the meat into pieces.
Cover the bottom of a very large (at least 20-quart) pot with vegetable oil.
Add the onions and peppers and cook over medium heat until softened.
Add the chicken and pork, and pour in enough chicken broth to cover. Cook for 15 minutes. Add the tomato sauce, bring to a boil, then reduce the heat to low.
Add the Worcestershire, corn, tomatoes, and lima beans.
Season to taste with salt and pepper, and simmer for 1 hour. Before serving, add hot sauce and dried hot peppers to taste.

SMOKED TURKEY

*Instead of using a whole turkey, try cutting it into serving pieces, and proceeding with the recipe.
When the turkey is placed in the smoker, add the breasts for the final 2 to 3 hours of smoking,
and remove them when their internal temperature is 160°F.*

1 turkey (8 to 10 pounds)
1 cup plus 3 tablespoons kosher salt
½ cup brown sugar
1 to 2 teaspoons dried red pepper flakes
6 garlic cloves, crushed
1 tablespoon fennel seed

Rinse the turkey and pat dry with paper towels. In a small bowl, combine
1 cup of the salt, the sugar, half the red pepper flakes, half the garlic, and half the fennel seed.
Rub the turkey generously inside and outside with the rub mixture. Place in a large plastic bag and
refrigerate for 12 to 24 hours. Rinse the turkey thoroughly and pat dry with paper towels.
Set it to dry on a rack in a well-ventilated area until the skin is glossy, about 4 hours.
You can place the turkey in front of a fan to hasten the process, but it will still take about 2 hours.
Rub the turkey with the remaining garlic. Crush the remaining fennel seed in a mortar,
and add the remaining salt and red pepper flakes. Mix well and rub on the outside of the turkey.
Preheat the smoker to 225°F with equal parts cherry and hickory wood. Place the turkey
in the smoker and smoke-cook until a meat thermometer in the thigh reads 170°F.

COOKSHACK SMOKED TURKEY

1 self-basting turkey (10 to 12 pounds)
2 apples, quartered
1 onion, quartered
Vegetable oil
Cookshack Spicy Chicken Rub

Rinse and dry the turkey. Stuff it with the apples and onions. Rub the turkey skin with vegetable oil and season with the chicken rub. Preheat the smoker to 225°F with 4 ounces of hickory wood. Place the turkey in the smoker and smoke-cook for 10 hours. Discard the stuffing before serving.

SMOKIN' OKIE TURKEY BRINE

This makes enough brine for a 10- to 12-pound turkey.
If you've never tasted a turkey that was brined before cooking, you'll be amazed at the moist, smooth texture of the meat.

1 gallon water
1 cup coarse kosher salt
¾ cup soy sauce
½ cup white sugar
½ cup brown sugar
½ cup honey
½ cup apple cider vinegar
4 tablespoons black pepper
3 to 4 tablespoons chopped garlic
1 ounce Morton's Tenderquick
1 teaspoon ground allspice

In a large nonreactive glass or stainless steel container, combine the water, salt, soy sauce, sugars, honey, vinegar, pepper, garlic, Tenderquick, and allspice. Add the turkey, making sure it's covered with brine, and refrigerate for 12 hours. Remove from the refrigerator and discard the brine. Rinse the turkey three times, and pat dry with paper towels. Smoke-cook as desired.

APPLE-SMOKED TURKEY

1 cup kosher salt
1 cup brown sugar
1 cup honey
½ cup minced garlic
½ cup coarsely ground black pepper
4 cinnamon sticks
1 gallon water
1 turkey (10 to 12 pounds)

In a large saucepan, combine the salt, sugar, honey, garlic, pepper, cinnamon, and water.
Bring to a boil over medium heat, stirring continuously. Remove from the heat and cool to room
temperature. Place the turkey in a large nonreactive glass or stainless steel container.
Add the brine, cover, and refrigerate for 24 to 36 hours. Preheat the smoker to 225°F with 4 ounces
of apple wood. Drain and rinse the turkey. Place in the smoker and smoke-cook for 6 hours.

SMOKED STUFFED TURKEY WITH ITALIAN SAUSAGE AND ONIONS

*Serve the turkey meat "pulled" from the carcass instead of slicing it.
The sausage may be sliced on the diagonal and served with the turkey.
The total smoking time should be 5 to 6 hours.*

1 turkey (10 to 12 pounds)
¼ cup Blackburn's Waffle Syrup
Garlic salt
Lemon pepper
½ pound mild Italian sausage, coarsely chopped
½ medium onion, coarsely chopped

Preheat the smoker to 250°F. Remove the neck and giblets from the turkey, rinse well, and drain. Rub the turkey skin with a thin layer of the waffle syrup. Coat the inside and outside of the turkey generously with garlic salt and lemon pepper. Insert the sausage and onion into the cavity. Place the turkey, breast side up, in a large aluminum pan. Place in the smoker and smoke for about 3 hours. Cover with heavy-duty foil, and return to the smoker until the internal temperature registers 180°F on a meat thermometer. Turn off the smoker and let the turkey cool slowly in the smoker. This slow cool-down actually increases tenderness, plus allows moisture to be drawn back into the meat. Remove foil. Drain off liquid for gravy if desired or simply discard.

LEMON-SMOKED TURKEY BREAST

¼ cup lemon juice
2 tablespoons vegetable oil
1 teaspoon dried dill
½ tablespoon paprika
½ tablespoon black pepper
½ tablespoon grated lemon zest
2 garlic cloves, chopped
4 pounds boneless turkey breast, skin removed
Vegetable cooking spray

In a small bowl, combine the lemon juice, vegetable oil, dill, paprika, pepper, lemon zest, and garlic, and stir to combine.
Rinse and dry the turkey breast. Trim off any fat and tendons.
Tuck the narrow end under the breast to create a uniform size, and tie the turkey securely with string at 2-inch intervals. Brush the turkey breast with the lemon juice mixture. Preheat the smoker to 225°F with 2 ounces of hickory wood and 1 garlic clove in the wood box. Coat the smoker rack with vegetable cooking spray and place the turkey breast on it. Smoke-cook for 5 hours, basting with the remaining lemon juice mixture after 3 hours.

SMOKED DUCK

*Try shredding or "pulling" the duck meat, then serve in warm tortillas with
black bean sauce, plum sauce, or even a good salsa with tomatillo.
Accompany with grilled asparagus, cold beer, and moon pies.*

DUCK AND BRINE:
2 cups iodine-free salt
1 gallon water
4 tablespoons minced garlic plus 2 whole garlic cloves
6 peppercorns
1 duck (3 pounds)
2 tablespoons julienne of ginger root

BASTING SAUCE:
1 cup soy sauce
2 cups water
2 tablespoons coarsely ground black pepper
4 tablespoons garlic powder
Juice of 1 lemon

In a large pot, combine the salt, water, garlic, and peppercorns. Bring to a boil, then cool.
Place in a large nonreactive glass or stainless steel container and add the duck.
Cover and refrigerate for 8 hours. Remove the duck from the brine, pat dry with paper
towels, and let it come to room temperature. Preheat the smoker to 210°F with cherry wood.
Cut the whole garlic cloves into slivers. Using a sharp knife, cut slits in the skin of the duck.
Insert the garlic and ginger into the slits in the duck skin. In a medium bowl, combine
the soy sauce, water, pepper, garlic powder, and lemon juice. Brush the mixture on the duck
and place, breast side up, in the smoker. Smoke, basting occasionally, until the internal
temperature reaches 160°F.

APPLE-SMOKED DUCKLING
WITH PLUM AND CHERRY CHUTNEY

1 duck (5 to 6 pounds)
Salt and pepper
1 apple, cut into 8 pieces
Plum and Cherry Chutney (recipe follows)

Rinse and dry the duck, removing all giblets from the cavity.
Trim off the neck, wings, and tail. Season the cavity with salt and pepper, and stuff it
with the giblets (except the liver), neck, wings, and apple pieces.
Preheat the smoker to 225°F with 2 ounces of apple wood. Place the duck in the smoker
and smoke-cook for 2½ hours. Remove the contents of the cavity and allow the duck to cool.
Cut the duck in half and carefully remove all bones except wing and leg bones.
Remove all excess fat. Reheat in a 400°F oven, and finish under the broiler until the skin is
crisp. Serve with Plum and Cherry Chutney.

Plum and Cherry Chutney
1 cup apple cider vinegar
¼ cup water
1 small yellow onion, finely diced
1 small green bell pepper, seeded and finely diced
2 cloves garlic, chopped
Salt to taste
1½ teaspoons mustard seeds
Pinch of grated fresh ginger
1 tablespoon orange marmalade
½ teaspoon cayenne pepper
⅛ teaspoon cinnamon
1½ cups packed brown sugar
½ cup sugar
⅓ cup dried cherries
⅓ cup dried currants
1 pound fresh plums, pitted and diced

In a large saucepan, combine the vinegar, water, onion, pepper, garlic, salt, mustard seeds, ginger,
marmalade, cayenne, and cinnamon and bring to a boil. Simmer, uncovered, for 15 to 20 minutes, or
until the onion is translucent. Add the sugars; bring back to a boil, then reduce the heat and simmer
for 1 hour. Add the cherries, currants, and plums. Cook for 15 minutes longer, or until thickened.
Cool before serving.

SMOKED DUCK BREASTS WITH JEZEBEL SAUCE

*Enjoy this tender smoked duck with sweet potato biscuits and tangy Jezebel sauce.
The 2000–2001 Recipe Contest first prize-winning recipe was submitted by
Corkey Bergamo. Morton's Tenderquick is a curing product that's
available from online butcher-shop sites.*

1 cup Morton's Tenderquick
1¼ cups brown sugar
1 gallon water
7 duck breasts (16 to 20 ounces each), skin on
Jezebel Sauce (recipe follows)

In a container large enough to hold all the duck breasts, combine the Tenderquick, sugar,
and water and mix well. Add the duck breasts, cover, and refrigerate for 24 hours.
Remove the duck from the brine and soak in cold water for 30 minutes.
Remove and pat dry. Place on racks and refrigerate overnight.
Preheat the smoker to 160°F with 4 ounces apple
wood. Smoke-cook the duck for 3 hours and 15 minutes. Remove from the smoker, let cool,
and chill. To serve, remove the skin and thinly slice on the diagonal.

Jezebel Sauce

*This is also delicious served over cream cheese with crackers, or as a sauce
for roast pork and pork tenderloin.*

½ cup prepared horseradish
1 cup pineapple preserves
1 cup apple jelly
1 teaspoon dry mustard

Drain the horseradish well by pressing between layers of paper towels.
Combine with the preserves, jelly, and mustard, mixing well.
Cover and refrigerate until ready to serve.

TEA-SMOKED DUCK ON A BED OF SWEET POTATO MASH

For the tea leaves, just tear open a few teabags and use the contents. Serve the sliced duck on a bed of mash, topped with the red wine sauce, with onion and broccoli on the side.

DUCK:
6 tablespoons brown sugar
¼ cup rice
¼ cup tea leaves
2 duck breasts

SWEET POTATO MASH:
1 large sweet potato, peeled and chopped
½ cup red wine
Salt to taste
2 tablespoons olive oil
½ red onion, peeled and cut into 6 wedges
2 teaspoons soy sauce
4 tablespoons unsalted butter

Line the bottom of a large sauté pan with foil. In a small bowl, combine 4 tablespoons of the sugar, the rice, and tea leaves, and pour on the foil. Cover the tea mixture with another piece of foil. Place the duck breast on the foil. Cover with a lid and cook over medium heat for 12 minutes, or until cooked through. Bring half a medium saucepan of salted water to a boil. Add the sweet potato and cook until tender. Drain and set aside. Pour the wine into a small saucepan and bring to a simmer over medium heat. Add the remaining sugar and stir until melted. Simmer for about 5 minutes, until thickened.
In a small skillet, warm the oil over medium heat.
Add the onion and sauté until softened and caramelized.
Using tongs, remove the duck from the pan. Slice on the diagonal.
Drain the potatoes and return to the saucepan. Add the soy sauce and mash until smooth. Whisk the butter into the red wine, and simmer gently until warmed through.
Serve the sauce with the duck and mashed sweet potatoes.

SMOKED BIRDS AND MEATS WITH HOMEMADE BAR-B-QUE SAUCE

2 gallons plus 2 cups water
2 cups canning salt
Poultry or meat of your choice
1 tablespoon rosemary
1 tablespoon caraway seed
1 tablespoon fennel seed
2 tablespoons fresh chopped garlic
4 bay leaves
2 cups dark brown sugar
Homemade Bar-B-Que Sauce (recipe follows)

Pour the 2 gallons of water into a 5-gallon pail and add the salt.
Add the poultry or meat of your choice, cover, and brine for 3 to 4 hours. In a small saucepan,
combine the rosemary, caraway, fennel, garlic, bay leaves, sugar, and remaining water.
Bring to a boil, remove from the heat, and steep for 20 minutes. Add to the meat or poultry
in the brine. Cover and refrigerate for at least 8 hours.
Preheat the smoker and add the meat or poultry. Smoke-cook for 5 to 6 hours.
Before serving, dip into Homemade Bar-B-Que Sauce.

Homemade Bar-B-Que Sauce
*This sauce can be used on all smoked, grilled,
or roasted meat and poultry.*

1 medium onion, chopped
2 tablespoons butter
2 tablespoons vinegar
2 tablespoons brown sugar
2 tablespoons lemon juice
⅛ teaspoon cayenne pepper
1 cup ketchup
3 tablespoons Worcestershire sauce
½ tablespoon black pepper
1 cup water
1 tablespoon celery salt

In a medium saucepan, combine the onion, butter, vinegar, sugar, lemon juice,
cayenne, ketchup, Worcestershire, pepper, water, and salt. Bring to a boil, remove from
the heat, and use as a basting sauce on smoked chicken or meat.

HONEY-SMOKED GOOSE

1 gallon water
1 cup kosher salt
2 tablespoons curing salt
½ cup Madeira wine
1 cup honey
Pinch of thyme
2 bay leaves
6 juniper berries
½ teaspoon black peppercorns
1 goose (6 to 8 pounds)

In a large pot, combine the water, salts, Madeira, honey, thyme, bay leaves, juniper berries, and peppercorns. Bring to a boil, then cool and strain into a large, nonreactive glass or stainless steel container. Add the goose, cover, and refrigerate for 48 hours.
Preheat the smoker to 225°F with 4 ounces of hickory wood.
Place the goose in the smoker and smoke-cook for 4 hours.

SMOKED QUAIL

8 to 10 quail or 2 pheasants, split
Cookshack Spicy Chicken Rub
1 onion, chopped
1 sweet red pepper, chopped
8 ounces heavy cream
1 can condensed cream of chicken soup
1 pound fresh mushrooms
¼ cup sherry or apple cider
⅛ teaspoon tarragon
⅛ teaspoon ground lemon peel
Salt and pepper to taste

Preheat the smoker to 225°F with 2 ounces of apple wood. Rub the quail or pheasants with chicken rub and place them in heavy aluminum foil pans. In a medium bowl, combine the onion, pepper, heavy cream, condensed soup, mushrooms, sherry, tarragon, lemon peel, salt, and pepper.
Mix well and pour over the quail. Cover loosely with foil, and punch several holes in the foil.
Place in the smoker and smoke-cook for 2 hours.

SMOKED PHEASANT

2 cups kosher salt
2 cups brown sugar
1 cup honey
1 cup molasses
4 cinnamon sticks
2 tablespoons minced garlic
½ cup apple juice concentrate
1 cup soy sauce
2 gallons water
2 pheasants (5 pounds each)

In a large nonreactive glass or stainless steel pot, combine the salt, sugar, honey, molasses, cinnamon, garlic, apple juice concentrate, soy sauce, and water. Bring to a boil. Remove from the heat and refrigerate until cool; do not place the pheasants in hot brine! After the brine has cooled, add the pheasants, cover, and refrigerate for 18 hours. Preheat the smoker to 225°F with 2 ounces of cherry wood. Place the pheasants in the smoker and smoke-cook for 3 hours.

SHELLFISH & SEAFOOD

JT'S SMOKED SEA BASS

This recipe is from Jason Fisherman of Newport Tradewinds in Newport, Oregon.

5 pounds fresh sea bass filets
1 cup salt
1 cup brown sugar
3 tablespoons plus 1 teaspoon of above mixture

Place the fish in a single layer in a large nonreactive glass or stainless steel pan. In a small bowl, combine the salt and sugar. Sprinkle 3 tablespoons plus 1 teaspoon of the cure mixture over the fish; reserve the remaining cure mixture for another time. Cover and refrigerate the fish for 24 hours. Preheat the smoker to 150° to 160°F. Add the fish and smoke for 6 to 8 hours, depending on the thickness of the filets.

GARLICKY SMOKED CLAM LINGUINE

This recipe from Lonnie Plenert works best if the clams are put into a cold smoker that's set to come up to temperature with the clams inside.

1 large (51-ounce) can chopped clams
½ cup olive oil
Seasoned salt to taste
4 tablespoons (½ stick) butter
9 large garlic cloves, finely chopped
½ cup dry white wine
2 large carrots, coarsely chopped
2 tablespoons dried oregano
1 pound linguine
Chopped parsley, for garnish

Prepare the smoker with 2 to 3 ounces of cherry wood, but do not preheat.
Drain the clams, reserving the liquid, and press to remove all excess liquid.
Spread on 2 smoker racks covered with foil, and drizzle with enough olive oil to lightly coat the clams. Sprinkle with the seasoned salt and toss thoroughly. Spread out and place in a smoker set to 175°F. Turn on the smoker and smoke for about 1 hour.
While the clams are smoking, heat the remaining olive oil and butter in a large skillet.
Add the garlic and sauté for about 2 minutes until fragrant. Add the wine, carrots, oregano, and reserved clam liquid. Boil until reduced to about 1½ cups. Add the smoked clams to the sauce.
Cook and drain the linguine. Serve with the clam sauce, garnished with chopped parsley.

PORTOBELLO MUSHROOMS WITH SMOKED CRAB IMPERIAL

2 portobello mushrooms, 5 to 6 inches in diameter
¼ pound crabmeat, drained and picked clean of shell pieces
1 green onion, chopped
1 tablespoon seasoned breadcrumbs
¾ tablespoon lemon juice
¾ tablespoon mayonnaise
¾ tablespoon Durkee seasoning sauce
½ teaspoon seasoned salt
⅛ teaspoon Cookshack Spicy Chicken Rub
Paprika

Rinse and dry the mushrooms thoroughly. Remove the stems and chop them coarsely.
Preheat the smoker to 200°F with 1 ounce of hickory or alder wood. Set the mushrooms on a
Cookshack seafood grill (or equivalent) and place in the smoker. Combine the crabmeat
and mushroom stems in a foil pan and place on the top grill of the smoker.
Smoke-cook for 1½ hours. Remove and cool.
Preheat a conventional oven to 400°F. In a medium bowl, combine the smoked crabmeat,
mushroom stems, green onions, breadcrumbs, lemon juice, mayonnaise, seasoning sauce,
seasoned salt, and chicken rub; mix well. Mound the crabmeat mixture into the mushroom caps.
Sprinkle with paprika. Bake for 15 minutes or until firm. Cool for 5 to 10 minutes.
Cut the stuffed mushrooms into wedges to serve as hors d'oeuvre on a bed of braised radicchio,
or serve as an entrée with asparagus and lemon-dill sauce.

MACADAMIA NUT-ENCRUSTED SALMON WITH CILANTRO RASPBERRY SAUCE

This recipe was submitted to Cookshack by Preston Davenport.

1 tablespoon sesame oil
1 tablespoon olive oil
1½ tablespoons grated ginger
1 tablespoon garlic powder
1 pound salmon filet
1 cup macadamia nuts, finely ground
½ cup grated Parmesan cheese
½ cup chopped scallions
3 tablespoons butter
½ cup chopped cilantro
½ cup raspberry jam

Preheat the smoker to 210°F. In a small bowl, combine 1 teaspoon of the sesame oil, 2 teaspoons of the olive oil, 1 teaspoon ginger, and 1 teaspoon of the garlic powder. Rub over the salmon and place in a heatproof pan. Combine the macadamia nuts, Parmesan, 1 teaspoon ginger, and 1 teaspoon garlic powder. Coat the salmon with the nut mixture. Place in the smoker and smoke-cook for 2½ hours. To prepare the sauce, combine the remaining sesame oil, olive oil, ginger, and scallions in a small sauté pan and cook over medium heat until the scallions begin to caramelize. Reduce the heat to low and stir in the butter, most of the cilantro, remaining garlic powder, ginger, and jam. To serve, spread the sauce on a serving plate. Place the salmon in the sauce and garnish with the remaining cilantro.

SMOKED SALMON

*To add a Cajun touch, substitute a crab boil mix such as Old Bay
or Zatarain's seasoning for the salt.*

½ cup kosher salt
¼ cup brown sugar
¼ cup granulated sugar
2 tablespoons coarsely ground black pepper
1 tablespoon white pepper
1 tablespoon cayenne pepper
1 salmon filet (1 to 3 pounds), skin on

In a small bowl, combine the salt, sugars, and peppers.
Rub generously over the salmon. Wrap in plastic wrap, and then in foil.
Place in a pan and refrigerate for 16 to 24 hours.
Preheat the smoker to 150°F with 6 ounces of apple wood. Rinse the salmon and
pat with paper towels. Place in the smoker and smoke for 5 hours.

COOKSHACK HOT-SMOKED SALMON

2 pounds salmon filet
½ cup Morton's Tenderquick
2 cups water
1 egg
½ cup packed brown sugar

Rinse and dry the salmon, leaving the skin on. Dilute Morton's Tenderquick in
the water in a plastic container, according to the package directions.
Place the unshelled egg in the brine solution. If it does not float, add enough additional Tenderquick
to make it float. Remove the egg from the brine solution and stir in the brown sugar. Add the
salmon, immersing it completely in the brine. Cover and refrigerate for 4 hours.
Remove the salmon, discarding the brine. Rinse the salmon and soak it in cold water
for 30 minutes. Remove from the water and pat dry. Place it in a plastic container
and refrigerate, uncovered, for 8 hours.
Preheat the smoker to 200°F with 1 ounce of hickory wood.
Place the salmon in the smoker and smoke-cook for 1½ hours. Serve hot or chilled.

UNCLE PERCY'S SLAP YO' GRANMA CAJUN SMOKED SALMON

This is great served hot from the smoker. It also freezes well, and makes a good appetizer served cold on Ritz crackers with cream cheese, caviar, capers, and chopped onion.

2 large salmon filets
Olive oil
Tony Cachere's Cajun Seasoning, or other spice blend
Cracked black pepper
Cayenne pepper
Lemon slices

Preheat the smoker to 160°F with hickory or oak. Coat the salmon liberally with olive oil. Place the salmon skin side down on a doubled sheet of foil and turn up the sides of the foil to form a shallow pan. Sprinkle with the Cajun seasoning, and peppers. Top with lemon slices and set in the smoker. Smoke for 4 to 8 hours, depending on the size and thickness of the filets. Cooking for a longer time over low heat produces the best results.

SMOKY SALMON

Morton's Tenderquick is a meat-curing product that's available at many online butcher-shop sites.

1 cup Morton's Tenderquick
7 cups water
1 cup apple juice
3 tablespoons brown sugar
1 tablespoon pickling spice
Salmon steaks, 1 inch thick, skin on

In a large nonreactive stainless steel container, combine the Tenderquick, water, apple juice, sugar, and pickling spice. Add the fish, making sure it is covered by the liquid. Cover and refrigerate for at least 18 hours but no longer than 24 hours, turning every 4 hours. Preheat the smoker to 150°F with apple wood. Remove the fish from the refrigerator 1 hour before smoking and remove from the brine to a rack. Set the fish in the smoker and smoke for 1 hour. Increase the temperature to 200°F and smoke for 1½ hours longer.

T-RAY'S SMOKED SALMON

½ gallon water
1 cup brown sugar
½ cup kosher salt
½ cup soy sauce
2 pounds boneless, skinless salmon filets

In a large nonreactive glass or stainless container, combine the water, sugar, salt, and soy sauce. Add the salmon, cover, and refrigerate for at least 8 hours. Remove from the brine, dry with paper towels, and refrigerate uncovered for 2 to 3 hours. Preheat the smoker to 175° to 200°F with hickory wood. Add the salmon and smoke-cook for 3 to 4 hours. Remove from the smoker, cool, and serve at room temperature.

COOKSHACK BARBEQUE SHRIMP NOUVELLE ORLEANS

*This recipe works for either shrimp or chicken. Try serving it with boiled new potatoes,
corn on the cob, and heads of roasted whole garlic.*

SERVES 4

1 medium sweet onion, red or white, sliced
2 tablespoons chili powder
1 tablespoon chopped fresh garlic
4 green onions, chopped
2 tablespoons vegetable oil or olive oil
1 pound (16 to 20) extra-large shrimp,
shelled and deveined
6 ounces beer
2 tablespoons butter
1 teaspoon Worcestershire sauce
Hot cooked rice

In a large nonreactive glass or stainless steel container, combine the onion, chili powder,
garlic, green onions, and oil. Add the shrimp, toss to coat well, cover,
and refrigerate for at least 8 hours.
Preheat the grill and the smoker. Place the shrimp in a foil pan and pour the beer
over the shrimp, tossing to coat well. Place the pan on the grill and grill the shrimp until done, about
3 minutes per side. Transfer the shrimp to the smoker and smoke for about 30 minutes.
Remove the shrimp to a serving plate. Whisk the butter and Worcestershire sauce into the
hot pan drippings and pour over the rice.

BIG SID'S GRILLED SHRIMP

*Use this formula in any quantity you desire. It's a very simple recipe, but one of the best
ways ever to cook shrimp. Onion and bell pepper can be substituted for the jalapeño and cheese.
This recipe is from Eddie Champagne Jr. of Big Sid's in Luling, Louisiana.*

Large shrimp, shelled
Cheddar cheese, cut in ½-inch strips
Jalapeño peppers, cut in ¼-inch strips
Sliced bacon

Preheat the grill to medium heat. Butterfly the shrimp and stuff each one with a piece of cheese and a piece of jalapeño. Wrap each shrimp with a slice of bacon, and secure with a toothpick. Grill the shrimp until the bacon is crisp.

SMOKED OYSTERS, SHRIMP, AND SCALLOPS

This smoked shellfish medley is great with corn on the cob.

SERVES 2 TO 3

¼ pound (1 stick) butter
3 garlic cloves, thinly sliced
1 pound large shrimp (25 per pound), peeled and deveined
1 pound large scallops (15 per pound)
2 pints shucked large oysters, such as bluepoints
Chopped fresh parsley

Preheat the smoker with apple or mesquite chips. Combine the butter and garlic in a large, shallow pan or disposable aluminum pan that fits inside the smoker. Add the shrimp and scallops and smoke for 5 minutes. Add the oysters, turn the shrimp and scallops, sprinkle with parsley, and smoke for 5 to 10 minutes more.

MESQUITE-SMOKED GOAT CHEESE SHRIMP WITH GARLIC TOMATO COULIS

Two or three shrimp make a great appetizer, says Doug Jones of Dallas, Texas, who created this recipe. He serves four to six shrimp as a main dish.

1 tablespoon olive oil
1 (28-ounce) can stewed tomatoes
2 tablespoons crushed garlic
3 tablespoons chopped cilantro
¼ teaspoon cayenne pepper

Salt and pepper
Juice of 1 lime
1 pound (18 to 24) large shrimp, peeled and butterflied
½ pound soft goat cheese
1 (8-ounce) package cream cheese, at room temperature

To make the coulis, heat the olive oil in a large saucepan over medium high heat.
Add the stewed tomatoes, 1 tablespoon of the garlic, 2 tablespoons of the cilantro, cayenne, and
salt and pepper to taste. Bring to a boil, then reduce the heat to low and simmer for 35
to 45 minutes, until thick. Keep warm, and stir in the lime juice just before serving. Preheat the
smoker to 225°F with 4 ounces of mesquite wood. Place the shrimp on a sheet of foil on
the top rack of the smoker and smoke for 20 minutes. Remove the shrimp and place them
on a baking sheet. Preheat the oven to 325°F. In a medium bowl, combine the goat cheese, cream
cheese, 1 tablespoon of the garlic, 1 tablespoon of the cilantro, and salt and pepper to taste.
Using a small spoon, place about 1 teaspoon of the goat cheese mixture in the center of
each butterflied shrimp. Bake for 10 minutes. To serve, spoon the warm tomato coulis in the center of
a serving plate and place the shrimp on top.

BASIL-CURED SMOKED SHRIMP

3 cups water
2 cloves garlic, minced
¼ cup chopped onion
1 lemon, sliced, plus 1 tablespoon fresh lemon juice
⅓ cup honey
½ teaspoon cayenne pepper
2 tablespoons salt
1½ pounds (26 to 30) medium shrimp, peeled and deveined
¼ pound (1 stick) butter, melted
2 tablespoons fresh basil, minced
1 tablespoon Cookshack Rib Rub

In a nonreactive glass or stainless steel bowl, combine the water, garlic, onion, sliced
lemon, honey, cayenne, and salt. Mix well. Add the shrimp, refrigerate, and marinate
for 30 to 40 minutes. Drain well and pat dry.
Preheat the smoker to 275°F with 2 ounces of mesquite wood. Combine the butter, basil, lemon
juice, and rib rub. Brush each shrimp with the butter mixture, and place it on the grill.
(Use the special Cookshack seafood grill if available.) Smoke-cook the shrimp for about 20 minutes.
Before serving, lightly brush them with the remaining butter mixture.

SMOKED SHRIMP SCAMPI

1 pound medium shrimp, in the shell
¼ pound (1 stick) butter
4 cloves garlic, minced
⅓ cup dry white wine
¼ teaspoon freshly ground pepper

Preheat the smoker to 225°F with 2 ounces of mesquite wood. Add the shrimp and smoke-cook for 45 minutes. Remove the shrimp from the smoker, and peel and devein them.
In a large skillet, melt the butter over medium heat. Add the garlic and shrimp and cook, stirring constantly, for 3 to 5 minutes or until the shrimp turn pink. Add the wine and pepper. Bring to a boil and cook for 30 seconds, stirring constantly. Remove from the heat and serve immediately.

SPICY SMOKED SHRIMP SCAMPI

1 pound medium shrimp, in the shell
Old Bay Seasoning
1 pound (4 sticks) butter
2 tablespoons minced garlic
1 teaspoon salt

Preheat the smoker to 225°F with 4 ounces of mesquite wood. Season the shrimp liberally with Old Bay Seasoning. Place in the smoker and smoke-cook for 45 minutes.
Remove the shrimp from the smoker, and peel and devein them. In a large skillet, combine the butter, garlic, and salt over low heat, stirring until the butter melts.
Serve the shrimp with the scampi sauce.

MESQUITE-SMOKED TUNA

This recipe was developed by Pete Rudow.

6 tuna steaks, cut 1 inch thick

DRY CURE:
1 cup kosher salt
½ cup brown sugar
1 to 2 teaspoons red pepper flakes

MARINADE:
3 garlic cloves, crushed
4 slices ginger, about ¼-inch thick, crushed
4 to 5 tablespoons lime juice (juice of 3 limes)
3 tablespoons maple syrup
2 tablespoons light soy sauce

Rinse the tuna and pat dry. In a small bowl, combine the salt, sugar, and red pepper flakes. Generously rub the mixture over the tuna. Wrap in plastic wrap and refrigerate for 2 hours. Soak a handful of mesquite chips in water.
Rinse the tuna to remove the curing mixture. Dry completely with paper towels.
In a small bowl, combine the garlic, ginger, lime juice, maple syrup, and soy sauce.
Place the tuna in a nonreactive glass or stainless steel container and add the marinade.
Cover with plastic wrap and refrigerate for 2 to 4 hours.
Preheat the smoker to 240°F. Drain the mesquite chips and place on the coals. Remove the tuna from the marinade. Set the tuna on the top rack of the smoker and smoke for 15 to 30 minutes (for an electric smoker) or 30 minutes to 1 hour (for a regular smoker). Check the tuna after about 10 minutes; be careful not to let it dry out.

HOT SMOKED TUNA

This is a hot smoke recipe that doesn't use a cure.
The fish is meant to be served warm from the smoker. The recipe calls for tuna loins,
but you can use nice thick tuna steaks with equally good results.

3 pounds tuna loin, 1 to 2 inches thick
½ cup soy sauce (preferably dark soy)
½ cup maple syrup
5 garlic cloves, crushed
Juice of 5 limes
1 teaspoon red pepper flakes

In a nonreactive glass or stainless steel container large enough to hold the tuna in a single
layer, combine the soy sauce, syrup, garlic, lime juice, and red pepper flakes.
Add the tuna, cover, and refrigerate for 1 hour. Preheat the smoker to 250°F with 1 ounce hickory,
alder, or cherry wood. Remove the tuna from the container and drain of excess marinade,
but don't pat it dry. Place on the top smoker racks and smoke until the internal temperature
reaches 140°F on a meat thermometer.

SUGAR-SMOKED TUNA

This recipe also works well with salmon steaks.

2 tablespoons brown sugar
1 teaspoon minced lemon zest
1 tablespoon raw rice
2 pieces fresh lemongrass, coarsely chopped
4 tuna steaks
Salt and pepper to taste
2 tablespoons olive oil

In a small bowl, combine the sugar, lemon zest, rice, and lemongrass.
Preheat the smoker to 275°F with the lemongrass mixture in the wood box. Lightly season
the tuna or salmon with salt and pepper, and brush with olive oil. Place the fish in the
smoker and smoke-cook for 30 to 40 minutes. Remove to a serving platter, brush with more
olive oil, and serve at once.

HICKORY-SMOKED TUNA WITH CHIPOTLE BUTTER SAUCE AND WILTED SPINACH

¼ cup freshly cracked black pepper
¼ cup coarse sea salt
⅓ cup chopped fresh chives
1 pound tuna loin, ½ inch thick
Wilted Spinach (recipe follows)
Chipotle Butter Sauce (recipe follows)

In a small bowl, combine the pepper, salt, and chives. Press the mixture into the tuna.
Wrap tightly in plastic wrap and let rest for 30 minutes. Preheat the smoker to 200°F with
2 ounces of hickory wood. Unwrap the tuna and place in the smoker.
Smoke-cook for 55 minutes. When the tuna has cooled, slice it thinly.
To serve, place 3 slices of tuna on each plate. Add some Wilted Spinach
and drizzle with the Chipotle Butter.

Wilted Spinach
2 tablespoons butter
2 cups fresh spinach
1 tablespoon minced garlic
Salt and pepper to taste
1 tablespoon fresh lemon juice

In a medium skillet, melt the butter over medium heat.
Add the spinach and garlic and sauté until the spinach is wilted.
Add salt, pepper, and lemon juice. Toss lightly.

Chipotle Butter Sauce
1 cup chardonnay or other dry white wine
1 tablespoon chopped shallots
1 tablespoon rice vinegar
½ pound (2 sticks) butter, softened
2 tablespoons finely chopped chipotle pepper

In a small saucepan, combine the chardonnay, shallots, and rice vinegar.
Cook over medium high heat until reduced to about 2 tablespoons.
Turn off the heat and whisk in the softened butter slowly. Add the chipotle and
let the sauce stand to reach full flavor.

HOT SMOKED SWORDFISH STEAKS IN CITRUS ESSENCE

4 swordfish steaks, 6 ounces each
¼ cup olive oil
Salt and pepper
1 cup fresh orange juice
¼ cup lemon juice
1 tablespoon sugar
Grilled orange sections, for garnish

Coat the swordfish steaks with olive oil, and sprinkle with salt and pepper.
Preheat the smoker to 180°F with 1 cup dried citrus rind, soaked in water for 20 minutes,
in the smoker box. Place the fish in the smoker and smoke-cook for 1 hour.
To make the citrus essence, combine the orange juice and lemon juice in a small saucepan.
Bring to a boil, reduce the heat to a simmer, and cook until reduced by half.
Stir in the sugar. To serve, drizzle 2 tablespoons of the citrus essence on each of four warm plates.
Place the swordfish in the center. Garnish with grilled orange sections.

HERB-SMOKED WALLEYE

*This recipe from Julie Wynn won second place in the wood-smoked foods
category in Cookshack's 2000–2001 Recipe Contest.*

2 to 3 pounds walleye filets
¼ pound (1 stick) butter
⅓ cup lemon juice
Dill weed
Cayenne pepper

Preheat the smoker to 225°F with pecan or apple wood. Place the walleye filets on a
nonstick, perforated grilling sheet. Melt the butter and add the lemon juice. Brush on the walleye.
Sprinkle generously with dill and then lightly with cayenne pepper. Before placing the fish
in the smoker, throw a good handful of mixed fresh herbs (rosemary, chives, basil, oregano, and
thyme) on the smoking wood. Smoke until the fish is opaque.

BIG SID'S GRILLED REDFISH

This recipe is from Eddie Champagne Jr. of Big Sid's in Luling, Louisiana.

1 whole redfish or other fish, such as red snapper
¼ cup (½ stick) butter
½ cup chopped green onions
1 tablespoon chopped garlic
1 tablespoon chopped fresh basil
Juice of ½ lemon
Salt, pepper, and cayenne pepper to taste
Lemon slices and parsley sprigs, for garnish

Preheat the grill to 225°F. Remove the filet from the fish, leaving the
scales on the filet. In a small saucepan, melt the butter and add the green onions.
Sauté briefly, then add the garlic, basil, lemon juice, salt, pepper, and cayenne. Place the fish, scale
side down, on the grill. Baste it frequently with the lemon butter and grill until the fish flakes
with a fork. Remove from the grill with a long spatula, and garnish with lemon and parsley.

BIG DADDY'S APPLE WOOD-SMOKED TROUT

Fresh trout
Apple juice
Grapeseed oil

Clean the trout, leaving the heads on. Place in a nonreactive glass or stainless steel
container and cover with apple juice. Cover and refrigerate for 2 to 3 hours.
Preheat the smoker to 225°F. Remove the trout and drain well. Brush the inside and outside
of the trout with the grapeseed oil. Place in the smoker and smoke-cook for 3 to 4 hours.

COOKSHACK SMOKED RAINBOW TROUT

2 whole rainbow trout (1 pound each)

Rinse and dry the trout. Preheat the smoker to 200°F with 1 ounce of hickory wood.
Place the unseasoned trout in the smoker and smoke-cook for 45 minutes.

HICKORY-SMOKED CAJUN CATFISH

¼ cup Cookshack Spicy Barbecue Sauce Mix
1 teaspoon white pepper
1 tablespoon Cajun seasoning
1 teaspoon cayenne pepper
2 whole catfish (2 to 3 pounds each)

In a small bowl, combine the barbecue sauce mix, pepper, Cajun seasoning, and cayenne. Rinse and dry the catfish. Rub the spice mixture evenly over the catfish, inside and outside. Preheat the smoker to 225°F with 2 ounces of hickory wood. Place the fish in the smoker and smoke-cook for 2 hours.

KATZEN DAWGS (CATFISH HUSH PUPPIES)

½ cup yellow or white cornmeal
½ cup flour
2 tablespoons baking powder
1 teaspoon baking soda
2 eggs
1 cup buttermilk or beer
1 tablespoon lemon juice
2 tablespoons bacon fat or melted shortening
1 teaspoon Tabasco
¾ cup thinly sliced green onions
1 pound smoked, peppered catfish filets, coarsely chopped
Peanut oil for frying
Tartar sauce

Sift the cornmeal, flour, baking powder, and baking soda into a large bowl. In a 2-cup glass measuring cup, beat the eggs. Add enough buttermilk or beer to measure 1¼ cups liquid. Add the lemon juice, bacon fat, and Tabasco. Let stand for 10 minutes. Stir the liquid ingredients into the cornmeal mixture. Fold in the green onions and catfish.
In a deep fryer or heavy skillet, heat at least 2 inches of oil to 365°F. Using two tablespoons, drop the batter, a spoonful at a time, into the hot oil. As the hush puppies rise to the surface, turn them to brown on all sides. Fry for 3 to 4 minutes, or until golden brown.
Drain on paper towels. Serve immediately with tartar sauce.

VEGETABLES

SMOKY SOW SANDWICH MARINATED COLESLAW

2 cups shredded cabbage
½ cup coarsely chopped Italian parsley
¼ cup julienne carrots
¼ cup sliced scallions
1 dill pickle, thinly sliced
⅓ cup freshly squeezed lime juice
1 tablespoon brown sugar
1 tablespoon vegetable oil
1 tablespoon Dijon mustard

In a medium bowl, combine the cabbage, parsley, carrots, scallions, pickle, lime juice, sugar, oil, and mustard. Mix well and refrigerate until ready to serve.

COLESLAW WITH A TWIST

2 (3-ounce) packages ramen chicken noodle soup mix
1 cup toasted, sliced almonds
1 cup roasted, salted sunflower seeds
1 pound bag broccoli coleslaw mix
1 bunch chopped green onions
2 cups chopped smoked turkey breast
½ cup confectioners' sugar
½ cup granulated sugar
⅓ cup cider vinegar
3 tablespoons sweet chili sauce

Crush the ramen noodles and reserve the flavor packets for the dressing. Place in a medium bowl and add the almonds and sunflower seeds. In a large bowl, combine the coleslaw mix and green onions. In a small bowl, combine the sugars, vinegar, and chili sauce, mixing well. Pour some over the coleslaw mix, tossing to combine. Add the noodle mixture and toss again, adjusting the dressing to taste. Top with the turkey, and chill until ready to serve.

APPLE-SMOKED PINTO BEANS

2 cups dried pinto beans
½ pound bacon, coarsely chopped
1 yellow onion, diced
2 quarts water
2 large garlic cloves, crushed
2 teaspoons chili powder
3 tablespoons brown sugar
1 beef bouillon cube
1 chicken bouillon cube

Pick over and rinse the pinto beans. Place the bacon in a large saucepan and cook until crisp. Add the onion and sauté until translucent. Add the pinto beans and 2 quarts of water, and bring to a boil. When most of the beans have floated to the top of the boiling liquid, turn the temperature down to a simmer. Add the garlic, chili powder, sugar, and bouillon cubes, and stir well. Preheat the smoker to 225°F with 1 to 2 ounces of apple or mesquite wood. Place the pan of beans in the smoker and smoke for 4 hours, until the beans are tender and the liquid has thickened. Alternatively, the beans can be simmered on the stovetop, uncovered, for 2 hours.

CHARRED VEGETABLE GRATIN

Chipotle peppers are smoked, dried jalapeño peppers. Smoke your own or find them in the Mexican food section of your supermarket. This recipe from Elaine Sweet won best of category for vegetables in the Cookshack 2000–2001 Recipe Contest.

8 plum tomatoes, halved lengthwise
1 Japanese eggplant, halved lengthwise
5 tablespoons olive oil
10 garlic cloves, coarsely chopped
1 teaspoon salt
2 tablespoons chopped fresh basil
1 tablespoon chopped fresh oregano
1 chipotle pepper, diced
6 tablespoons sour cream

Preheat the smoker to 225°F. Lightly brush the cut surfaces of the tomatoes and eggplant with olive oil and place, cut side down, in the smoker. Place the chopped garlic in a small baking dish and set it next to the vegetables. Smoke for 50 minutes.

Place the smoked tomatoes in a shallow serving bowl. Peel the eggplant and cut it into large cubes. Add the eggplant and garlic to the tomatoes. Season with salt and add the chopped basil and oregano. Add the chopped chipotle pepper and toss well. Serve warm, topped with sour cream.

WINTRY SMOKED ACORN SQUASH

This recipe from John Patterson took second place in the Winter 2001 National Barbecue Association contest.

5 cups apple cider
2 tablespoons brown sugar
2 teaspoons cinnamon, plus more for serving
2 medium acorn squash, halved and seeded
2 tablespoons butter

In a large saucepan, combine the cider, sugar, and 2 teaspoons of the cinnamon. Bring to a boil, then reduce the heat and simmer until the sugar is melted. Let cool. Place the squash in two heavy, zipper-lock plastic bags. Pour in the cider mixture, seal, and marinate for at least 2 hours at room temperature.

Preheat the smoker to 225°F with 2 ounces of hickory wood. Remove the squash from the bags, discard the marinade, and place the squash in the smoker, cut sides up. Divide the butter between the squash halves and smoke for 3 hours. Serve with cinnamon to taste.

SMOKY GRILLED TERIYAKI VEGETABLES

*Serve these as a side dish for steak, or assemble them into a
wonderful roasted veggie sandwich.*

1 eggplant, sliced ½ inch thick
2 red bell peppers, halved and seeded
2 yellow bell peppers, halved and seeded
2 zucchini, sliced
2 large onions, peeled and sliced ½ inch thick
¼ cup vegetable oil
1 cup teriyaki sauce

Preheat the smoker to 160°F with alder or apple wood. Brush the vegetables with
oil to coat, and place in a single layer on the smoker racks. Smoke for about
45 minutes. Preheat the grill to high heat. Brush the grate with oil. Arrange the vegetables on
the grill grate, with the peppers around the edges. Grill for 10 to 15 minutes,
turning once and basting frequently with the teriyaki sauce. The vegetables will cook at
different rates, so watch carefully and remove pieces as they are done.

SMOKY POTATO SALAD

This recipe from Regina Fisher won second place in the vegetable category in Cookshack's 2000–2001 Recipe Contest.

6 medium potatoes
2 eggs
¾ cup mayonnaise
1 tablespoon brown mustard
1 celery stalk, chopped
1 tablespoon sweet pickle relish
½ onion, diced
1 teaspoon salt
1 teaspoon pepper
1 teaspoon paprika

Preheat the smoker to 225°F with cherry wood. Leaving the skins on, cut the potatoes into quarters. Smoke-cook for 45 minutes, or until the potatoes are fork tender. While the potatoes are smoking, hard-boil the eggs. Let cool, shell, and dice them. Remove the skins from the potatoes and allow them to cool. Dice and place in a large bowl, Add the eggs, mayonnaise, mustard, celery, pickle relish, onion, salt, and pepper. Mix well. Sprinkle with paprika before serving.

SMOKED BAKED POTATOES

4 large baking potatoes
Olive oil
1 pound smoked brisket or smoked pork butt, chopped
Cookshack Spicy Barbecue Sauce
Sour cream

Rinse and dry the potatoes. Rub with olive oil. Preheat the smoker to 250°F with 6 ounces of mesquite wood. Place the potatoes in the smoker and smoke-cook for 4 hours. Remove from the smoker. Partially slice through the potatoes and open them up. Fill with the chopped smoked meat, and top with barbecue sauce and sour cream.

SMOKED LOADED POTATOES

5 large potatoes
Olive oil
Kosher salt
2 cups chopped smoked beef brisket
2 cups cooked broccoli florets
Cookshack Spicy Barbecue Sauce
Sour cream

Rinse and dry the potatoes. Rub with olive oil and roll in kosher salt.
Preheat the smoker to 250ºF. Place the potatoes in the smoker and smoke-cook for 3 hours.
Remove the potatoes from the smoker and partially slice through the potatoes to open
them up. Fill with the brisket and broccoli, and top with barbecue
sauce and sour cream to taste.

SMOKED MUSHROOMS AND VEGGIES

Serve these savory vegetable skewers with any smoked meat.

2 packages mixed wild mushrooms
1 package white button mushrooms
2 packages portobello mushrooms
2 large onions
½ pound plum tomatoes
3 tablespoons olive oil
1 tablespoon Cajun seasoning
3 garlic cloves, crushed

Wipe all the mushrooms. Slice the larger ones, and leave the small ones whole.
Quarter the onions. Alternate the mushrooms, onions, and plum tomatoes on skewers.
Brush with the olive oil and sprinkle with the Cajun seasoning and garlic. Preheat the smoker to
225°F. Smoke the vegetable skewers for 20 to 25 minutes.

SMOKED OLIVE OIL-POACHED TOMATOES

4 plum tomatoes
10 sprigs Italian parsley
1 bay leaf
2 sprigs thyme
1 tablespoon chopped basil
1 sprig oregano
2 garlic cloves
Salt and pepper
About 1 cup olive oil
8 (2½ inches thick) slices Italian bread

Preheat the smoker to 200°F with oak wood. Cut the tops off the tomatoes and place them in a heatproof bowl just large enough to hold the tomatoes. Tuck the parsley, bay leaf, thyme, most of the basil, oregano, and garlic between the tomatoes, and season with salt and pepper. Add enough olive oil to cover the tomatoes by ½ inch. Place the tomatoes in the smoker and smoke for 10 hours. Preheat the grill. To serve, grill each side of the bread quickly, then brush generously with some of the olive oil from the tomatoes. Top each slice of bread with a peeled tomato, sprinkle with the remaining chopped basil, and season to taste with salt and pepper.

SMOKED CORN ON THE COB
WITH SOUTHWEST BBQ BUTTER

4 ears of corn, in husks
1 cup Cookshack Spicy Barbecue Sauce
½ pound (2 sticks) butter
2 tablespoons Southwest Seasoning (see page TK)

Remove all but 2 layers of husks from the corn, and pull out the cornsilk. Preheat the smoker to 225°F with 2 ounces of hickory wood. Place the corn in the smoker and smoke-cook for 2 hours. In a small saucepan, combine the barbecue sauce, butter, and seasoning. Warm over medium heat, stirring constantly, until the butter is melted. Remove the remaining husks from the corn, and serve with the butter sauce.

DESSERTS

INDIAN PUDDING WITH SMOKED PEACH SAUCE

This recipe from Andi Flanagan took top prize in the dessert category in Cookshack's 2000–2001 Recipe Contest. If desired, it can be baked in a decorative mold pan. Unsweetened whipped cream makes a great topping.

4 cups milk
½ cup yellow cornmeal
⅓ cup light brown sugar
⅓ cup granulated sugar
⅓ cup molasses
1 teaspoon salt
5 tablespoons butter
1 teaspoon ground allspice
1 (16-ounce) can peach halves in heavy syrup, drained,
with 2 tablespoons syrup reserved
1 tablespoon lemon juice

Preheat the oven to 275°F. In a large, heavy saucepan, heat 2 cups of the milk until almost boiling. Slowly pour in the cornmeal, stirring constantly. Cook over very low heat, stirring constantly, for 10 to 15 minutes, until the cornmeal is creamy. Add the sugars, molasses, salt, butter, and allspice, and mix well. Pour into a well-buttered 1½-quart baking dish and pour the remaining milk over the top. Set into a larger pan containing enough hot water to come halfway up the sides of the baking dish. Bake for 3 hours. Remove from the water bath and let cool on a rack until firm. Preheat the smoker using pecan shells or hickory wood. To make the peach sauce, spread the drained peaches in a disposable aluminum pie plate and smoke for 25 minutes. Puree in a blender with the reserved syrup and the lemon juice.
Serve hot over the cooled pudding.

TIPSY PEACH TORTILLA NAPOLEONS

This recipe from Diane Sparrow won second place in the dessert category in the 2000–2001 Cookshack Recipe Contest.

4 firm ripe peaches
6 tablespoons butter, melted
¾ cup pecan halves
1 tablespoon sugar
4 flour tortillas

2 tablespoons cocoa
3 tablespoons sugar
2 tablespoons brown sugar
½ teaspoon cinnamon
¼ teaspoon nutmeg
3 tablespoons bourbon
4 scoops good quality vanilla ice cream

Pit the peaches and lay in a shallow pan. Brush the cut surfaces with
1 tablespoon of the melted butter. Toss the pecan halves in 2 tablespoons of the melted butter
and then toss in the sugar. Place the pecans in another shallow pan. Place the peaches
and pecans in the smoker and smoke-cook with apple or cherry wood for 30 minutes.
While the peaches and pecans smoke, brush the tortillas with 1 tablespoon melted butter
and sprinkle with cocoa and sugar. Cut each tortilla into quarters.
Place on a baking sheet and bake in a preheated oven for 3 minutes. Flip over and bake for
another 3 minutes. Remove from the oven and let cool. Place the remaining
2 tablespoons of butter in a small pan over medium heat. Add the brown sugar, cinnamon,
and nutmeg. Slice the smoked peaches into the butter mixture.
Add the bourbon and heat through. To serve, lay one of the cooled tortillas on each
of four serving plates. Spoon on some of the smoked peach mixture.
Top with another tortilla and more peaches. Continue stacking, ending with a tortilla.
Top with a scoop of vanilla ice cream and sprinkle with the smoked pecans.

SUGAR-SMOKED FRUIT TACOS

The fruit in this recipe is smoked over brown sugar.

2 (8-ounce) cans pineapple pieces, drained
2 bananas, sliced
½ cup plus 2 tablespoons dark brown sugar
4 tablespoons butter
1½ tablespoons confectioners' sugar
8 corn tortillas
3 cups unsweetened whipped cream
⅓ cup grated semisweet chocolate

Place the pineapple and bananas in a nonstick frying pan.
Sprinkle with 2 tablespoons of the brown sugar and cook over medium heat until the
fruit begins to brown. Transfer to a disposable aluminum pie plate. Form a sheet of
heavy-duty foil into a small cup for the remaining brown sugar, and place in the smoker wood box.
Heat the smoker to 150°F. As soon as smoking begins, place the pan with the fruit

into the smoker and smoke until the sugar has been used up. Remove the pan and let cool. Meanwhile, place 1 tablespoon of the butter and ½ tablespoon of the confectioners' sugar in a frying pan just big enough to hold one tortilla. Set over medium heat and cook, stirring, until the sugar melts. Add a tortilla and cook for about 30 seconds. Turn and cook on the other side until browned and slightly crisp. Repeat with the remaining tortillas, adding more butter and sugar as needed. Fill each tortilla with the smoked fruit, top with whipped cream and grated chocolate, fold, and serve.

POMEPOSTEROUS

4 large apples (preferably Granny Smith or Red Delicious)
2 teaspoons lemon juice
2 Bosc pears, peeled
2 ounces brandy
½ cup dark brown sugar
1 teaspoon cinnamon
¼ teaspoon ground cloves
4 slices cheddar or Gouda cheese

Preheat the smoker with charcoal and hickory or mesquite chips.
Core the apples, leaving the bottoms intact, and sprinkle the insides with the lemon juice. Chop the pears into ½-inch pieces. In a small saucepan over medium heat, combine the brandy, sugar, cinnamon, and cloves, stirring until the sugar melts. Add the pears and stir to combine. Stuff the apples with the pear mixture and place in a disposable aluminum pie pan, or wrap the lower part of each apple with foil. Smoke for 2 to 3 hours, until the apples are soft. Top each apple with a slice of cheese 5 minutes before removing from the smoker, and smoke until the cheese begins to melt.

SMOKED CHEDDAR AND APPLE PIE WITH SMOKED GLAZED PECANS

½ pound cheddar cheese
2 cups pecans
6 tablespoons honey
1½ teaspoons cinnamon
1 (8-ounce) package cream cheese, at room temperature
1 cup sugar
1 egg, beaten
½ teaspoon vanilla
½ cup brown sugar
2 tablespoons lemon juice
2 tablespoons flour
¼ teaspoon nutmeg
¼ teaspoon salt
4 pounds Granny Smith apples, peeled, cored, and thinly sliced
Unbaked crust for 1 large deep-dish pie

Preheat the smoker to 175°F with 2 ounces of apple wood.
Place the cheese directly on the top rack of the smoker. Place the pecans in a disposable aluminum
pan and place on the bottom rack. Fill another disposable aluminum pan with ice and place
on the bottom rack. When you see smoke coming out the vent hole in a steady stream,
turn off the smoker. After 1 hour, taste a pecan to see if it needs more smoke flavor; if so,
repeat the cold-smoking process. Thinly slice the cheddar cheese.
Preheat the oven to 375°F. Put the smoked pecans on a baking sheet and toss with the honey
and ½ teaspoon of the cinnamon. Bake for 25 to 30 minutes, until lightly toasted. When cool,
chop 1½ cups of the pecans and set aside the remaining whole nuts. Leave the oven on.
In a large bowl, combine the cream cheese, ½ cup of the sugar, egg, and vanilla.
Beat until smooth and creamy. In another bowl, combine the remaining ½ cup of sugar, brown
sugar, lemon juice, flour, the remaining cinnamon, nutmeg, and salt.
Toss in the apples and chopped nuts and allow to rest for about 15 minutes.
Spread the cream cheese mixture on the bottom of the piecrust. Cover with a layer of
sliced smoked cheddar, and top with a layer of the apple mixture. Repeat with layers of
the cheddar and apple mixture until the crust is very full (the filling will decrease
in height as it bakes). Bake for 50 to 60 minutes, until the crust is lightly browned
and the apple mixture is bubbly. Garnish with the whole glazed pecans.
Serve warm with whipped cream or vanilla ice cream.

SMOKED BANANAS FOSTER PROVENÇAL

6 tablespoons butter
4 bananas, peeled and sliced lengthwise
1 teaspoon cinnamon
¼ cup brown sugar
1 cup chopped pecans
1 tablespoon heavy cream
½ cup spiced rum
4 tablespoons banana liqueur
4 scoops vanilla ice cream

Preheat the smoker to 210°F with apple wood. Butter a 9-x-14-inch baking pan. Line the bottom of the pan with thin slices of the banana. Place small pieces of the remaining butter over the bananas. Sprinkle evenly with the cinnamon, sugar, and chopped pecans. Place the pan in the smoker and smoke for about 1 hour, checking occasionally to ensure the mixture is not burning. The bananas should cook down, the butter melt, and the sugar begin to caramelize; if not ready after 1 hour, continue to smoke but do not add more wood. Pour the cream into a large sauté pan set over medium heat. Cut the bananas into pieces and add to the cream. Scrape the remaining caramel from the baking pan. Add the rum and liqueur to the baking pan, scraping up any caramel with a wooden spoon, and pour into the sauté pan, stirring frequently until warmed through. To serve, spoon the bananas over scoops of vanilla ice cream. If desired, carefully ignite the mixture so the alcohol flames briefly for a dramatic effect.

MESQUITE-SMOKED PEARS DELIGHT

This is very convenient to make if you're already smoking meat for a meal.

4 ripe Anjou pears
½ cup Hershey's chocolate shell
2 tablespoons plus 2 teaspoons raspberry
or boysenberry syrup
½ cup chopped nuts
1 cup whipped cream

Preheat the smoker to 200° to 250°F with about 2 ounces of mesquite wood.
Peel and core the pears, and cut in half lengthwise. Place in the smoker, cut side down, and smoke
for 20 minutes. Remove and let cool. Place each half, cut side down, in a small serving bowl.
Slowly spoon a tablespoon of the Hershey's chocolate shell on each half. Place in the refrigerator
for at least 1 hour. To serve, drizzle each half with a teaspoon of the raspberry syrup, sprinkle with
1 tablespoon chopped nuts, and top with whipped cream.

SMOKED ALMOND SHORTCAKE RINGS

*The "doughnut" holes left over after these cookies have been cut can also be baked,
making a tasty snack for the cook.*

MAKES ABOUT 20 COOKIES

¾ cup butter
½ cup confectioners' sugar
⅓ cup sour cream
2 cups flour
Milk, for brushing
⅓ cup chopped, blanched, smoked almonds

In a large bowl, combine the butter and sugar and cream until smooth.
Stir in the sour cream. Gradually stir in the flour. Gather and shape the dough into a ball,
and wrap in plastic. Refrigerate for several hours. Preheat the oven to 400°F.
Roll out the dough ½ inch thick. Cut into rings, using a doughnut cutter if available.
Place the rings 1 inch apart on an ungreased baking sheet. Brush with milk
and sprinkle with the smoked almonds. Bake for 10 to 12 minutes, or until the rings are light
golden brown. Cool on wire racks.

SMOKED SAUSAGE CAKE

This cake is outstanding with vanilla sauce or orange sauce,
or spread with marmalade.

1 pound mild bulk sausage
1 cup sultanas or golden raisins
½ cup very hot coffee
1½ cups sugar
1½ cups packed brown sugar
2 large eggs, beaten
3 cups flour
1 teaspoon ground ginger
1 teaspoon baking powder
1 teaspoon pumpkin pie spice
1 teaspoon baking soda
½ cup cold, strong coffee
1 cup chopped walnuts

Preheat the smoker to 100°F. Spread the sausage loosely on a pie plate and place on the top rack of the smoker. Smoke for 20 minutes, then remove and cool.
Place the sultanas in a small bowl, and cover with the hot coffee. Let the mixture sit while you prepare the cake. Preheat the oven to 350°F. In a large bowl, combine the sausage, sugars, and eggs, and beat well. In another bowl, combine the flour, ginger, baking powder, and pie spice.
Drain the coffee from the sultanas into the cold coffee, and stir in the baking soda. Add alternately to the sausage mixture with the dry ingredients, and mix well. Fold in the sultanas and walnuts. Turn into a 9-inch buttered and floured bundt pan. Bake for 1½ hours, or until a toothpick inserted into the center comes out clean. Cool in the pan for 15 minutes, then turn out onto a rack to cool.

SMOKED ALMOND AND APPLE BARS

1½ cups whole blanched almonds

CRUST:
½ cup vegetable shortening
¼ cup sugar
1 teaspoon vanilla extract
½ teaspoon almond extract
1 cup flour

FILLING:
2 large eggs
1 cup packed brown sugar
⅓ cup apple brandy, apple juice, or cider
2 teaspoons vanilla extract
⅓ cup flour
½ teaspoon baking powder
¼ teaspoon salt
5 Granny Smith apples, peeled, chopped, and tossed
with 1 tablespoon lemon juice to prevent discoloring

Preheat the smoker to 200°F with a handful of hickory chips.
Place the almonds in an aluminum pie plate punched full of holes. Place in the smoker
and smoke for 30 minutes. Let cool and coarsely chop the almonds.
Preheat the oven to 350°F. To make the crust, combine the shortening, sugar, and
extracts in a large bowl and cream together until smooth. Add the flour and mix well.
Press into the bottom of a greased 9-inch square pan. Bake for 15 minutes,
or until very lightly browned.

To make the filling: Combine the eggs and brown sugar in a large bowl and mix
until very thick. Add the brandy and vanilla and mix well. In another bowl, combine
the flour, baking powder, and salt. Slowly add to the egg mixture, beating well.
Fold in the apples and almonds. Spread over the cooled crust and bake for 25 minutes,
or until the filling is set. Cool in the pan on a rack and cut into bars to serve.

APPLE, ORANGE, AND SMOKED PECAN PIE

Try this pie topped with vanilla ice cream for delectable pie à la mode.

1½ cups pecan halves
5 cups peeled, roughly chopped Granny Smith apples
½ cup good quality orange marmalade
¾ cup sugar
¼ cup packed brown sugar
3 tablespoons flour
1 teaspoon ground cinnamon
Pastry for a two-crust, 9-inch pie

Preheat the smoker to 200°F with less than 1 ounce of hickory wood.
Place the pecans in an aluminum pie plate with holes punched all over the bottom.
Set the pan on the top rack of the smoker and smoke for 25 minutes. Add one cup
of the chopped apples, and smoke for 15 minutes longer. Transfer the mixture to a food
processor, add the remaining apples, and process to chop finely. Add the marmalade,
sugars, flour, and cinnamon, and process to combine. Preheat the oven to 375°F. Pour the
filling into a pie plate lined with a bottom crust. Top with the second crust and bake for
about 1 hour.

BREAD PUDDING

You can serve this hot or cold, with the topping of your choice.
Try it with maple syrup.

10 slices day-old bread, torn into pieces
1 quart milk, scalded
1 cup sweetened condensed milk
4 eggs
1 cup sugar
1 teaspoon cinnamon
½ teaspoon cloves
½ teaspoon nutmeg
½ teaspoon vanilla
¼ cup melted butter

Butter a 2-quart baking dish and preheat the oven to 350°F. In a large bowl, combine the bread, scalded milk, and condensed milk. In a separate bowl, beat the eggs, add the sugar, and mix well. Stir the egg mixture into the bread mixture and add the cinnamon, cloves, nutmeg, vanilla, and melted butter. Pour into the prepared dish and bake for 1 hour.

APPENDIX

TIPS FOR GOOD SMOKING

ADVANTAGES OF SMOKE-COOKING IN A COOKSHACK:

✻ Slow smoke-cooking draws out fat and seals in juices. Heat and smoke cause the meat fibers to break down, which releases the fat while tenderizing the cut. Low cooking temperatures prevent moisture from escaping as steam.

KEEP YOUR SMOKER CLEAN

✻ Keep your SUPER SMOKER well seasoned and clean. Keep it free of excess grease, smoke buildup and scale! A dirty smoker will transfer unpleasant odors and tastes to the product. Follow the cleaning instructions found in your Cookshack Operator's Manual carefully. An added bonus of a clean smoker: Heating elements will last longer and you will save money.

RECIPE CONVERSION:

✻ When converting conventional recipes: Smoke-cook product for twice the recommended time at three-fourths of the temperature. For example, if your conventional recipe says to cook product for 3 hours at 350° F, smoke-cooking would take approximately 6 hours at 260° F.

PREHEATING OF SMOKER:

✻ Cooking times are calculated from the time the smoker is turned on. **Do not preheat the smoker unless preheating is specified in a particular recipe.**

SEASONINGS:

✻ Try lots of seasonings, such as traditional barbecue spices, Tex-Mex, Caribbean, Cajun and Oriental. All these zesty tastes work wonderfully well with smoked foods. Experiment and find flavors that your customers like.

STEAM HEAT:

✻ Smoked foods and steam are not friends. Steam causes smoke flavor to disappear rapidly and the texture of smoked meats to go soggy. **Avoid steam.**

Meat Thermometer:

★ Use a meat thermometer to determine the internal temperature of smoked product. Oven temperature is not an accurate indicator of doneness. Smoke-cooking times are not as precise as conventional oven cooking times.

Slow Cooking Without Smoke:

★ Your smoker, without wood, is an excellent slow-cook and hold oven. Use it for slow-roasting meats and poultry. Cooking times are the same as for smoke-cooking.

Low-Fat Cooking:

★ Fat drips from meat as it smoke-cooks in the smoker, so there is less fat in the finished product. Choose cuts of meat with less fat. Cover the vent hole of your smoker to raise humidity while smoke-cooking. Trim fat from smoked product before serving.

★ Fish and chicken are low-fat alternatives that smoke very well. Smoke-cook skinless, boneless chicken breasts (45 minutes for 6-ounce breasts), sprinkle with Parmesan cheese while hot and serve immediately.

★ Cover fish filets or steaks with fresh dill. Smoke-cook according to general instructions in Fish and Seafood section. Squeeze on lemon or lime juice just before serving. Garnish with dill and lemon or lime slices.

Low-Salt Cooking:

★ Low salt doesn't have to be low flavor when you smoke. Experiment with different salt-free seasonings. Add herbs, spices, tea leaves or citrus peels to the woodbox for more flavor.

Precise Cooking Times:

★ Many of the recipes in this book do not have precise cooking times specified. Smoke-cooking is not an exact science, and when smoking at low temperatures, a few minutes more or less usually does not affect the quality of the product.

★ Other variables, such as temperature of product going into the smoker, size, weight and mass of the product, etc., also affect cooking time.

★ Just follow the guidelines provided. Use your common sense, be prepared to experiment a bit and you'll get the results you want. While these recipes and processing information are both accurate and feasible to the best of our knowledge, Cookshack, Inc. cannot accept any responsibility or liability for product failure or lack of acceptance.

WOOD:

✻ What kind of wood and how much you use for flavoring are a matter of personal taste. Your Cookshack Operator's Manual will tell you the maximum amount of wood that your smoker can safely use. **Do not exceed this amount.**

GENERAL TIPS:

✻ Run racks and grills through the dishwasher. It's the easiest way to clean them.

✻ Buy a flat-bladed paint scraper and hang it on the wall near your smoker. Use it to scrape down the walls after cooking.

✻ Keep an extra fork and tongs near the smoker.

✻ Spray grills with a vegetable oil spray to prevent sticking.

✻ If you don't have a foil pan recommended for cooking certain items, make a "boat" by folding up edges of aluminum foil.

TIME AND TEMPERATURE CHART:

✻ "Per lb." refers to the average weight of individual pieces, not the weight of the entire load.

PRODUCT	COOKING TIME	OVEN TEMPERATURE
Beef brisket	1 hour per lb. 10 hour minimum	200° F
Prime rib	5 hours for a 12-lb. rib cooked to medium-rare	200° F
Pork ribs	1 hour per lb.	230° F
Pork roast	1 hour per lb. 4 hour minimum	200° F
Chicken	1 hour per lb.	225° F
Turkey	10 hours for a 12-lb. turkey	180° to 200° F

✻ Always cook product to safe internal temperatures. Verify temperatures with a meat thermometer. If in doubt, contact your local health department.

INTERNAL TEMPERATURE CHART

★ The temperatures shown are those recommended by the USDA (United States Department of Agriculture) and FDA (Food and Drug Administration) as internal temperatures to which meat, poultry and seafood should be cooked. They do not refer to oven temperatures.

PRODUCT	INTERNAL TEMPERATURE
Beef	155° F
Ground Beef	In February, 1993, the FDA issued interim guidance to food service operators that ground beef should be cooked to 155° F. Juices should run clear and all pink color on the inside should be gone.
Pork	160° F for medium 170° F for well done
Veal	160° F for medium 170° F for well done
Lamb	160° F for medium 170° F for well done
Chicken	180° F Juices should run clear when skin is pierced with a fork.
Turkey	180° F Juices should run clear when skin is pierced with a fork. Turkey breasts may be safely cooked to an internal temperature of 170° F. Cook thighs and wings until the juices run clear.
Fish	Smoke-cook fish for 1 hour per pound of thickness. Add 1/2 hour to smoke-cook time for frozen fish.

GUIDE TO BRINING AND SMOKING

MEAT/POULTRY:

ITEM	BRINING METHOD	BRINING TIME	SMOKING TIME	TO FINISH
Whole boneless 2- to 4-lb. cuts of pork, beef or lamb	Wet brine	6 to 8 hours	6 to 8 hours	Brush pork with oil; roast at 375° F until meat thermometer inserted into thickest part registers 150° F (15 minutes per pound). Brush beef or lamb with oil; roast at 375° F until meat thermometer inserted into thickest part registers 130° F (10 minutes per pound for medium-rare).
Pork or lamb chops, or beef steaks, 1-inch thick	Wet brine	4 hours	3 hours	Sauté or grill pork chops until cooked through, 3 to 4 minutes per side; sauté or grill lamb chops or beef steaks for 3 minutes per side for medium-rare.
Whole 8- to 10-lb. turkey	Wet brine	12 hours	6 hours	Brush with oil; roast at 350° F until meat thermometer inserted into thickest part of thigh registers 165° F (10 minutes per pound).
Whole 3- to 4-lb. chickens or ducks	Wet brine	8 hours	4 hours	Brush with oil; roast at 350° F until meat thermometer inserted into thickest part of thigh registers 165° F (10 minutes per pound).
Boneless 6- to 8-oz. chicken or duck breasts, skin on	Wet or dry brine	Wet brine 4 hours or dry brine 1 hour	3 hours	Brush with oil; sauté or grill for 3 to 4 minutes per side or until cooked through.

Guide to Brining and Smoking

Fish/Shellfish:

ITEM	BRINING METHOD	BRINING TIME	SMOKING TIME	TO FINISH
Whole 3- to 4-lb. salmon filets, skin on, or 6-oz. salmon steaks	Wet brine	8 hours for filets; 1 hour for steaks	6 hours for filets; 2 hours for steaks	Brush filets with oil; bake at 350° F for 5 minutes or until opaque throughout. Grill steaks for 2 to 3 minutes per side or until opaque throughout.
Thin fish filets, such as sole or snapper, or small, whole fish	Sprinkle with dry brine	0	2 hours	Sauté or grill the fish for 2 minutes per side or until opaque throughout.
Large scallops	No brining	0	1½ hours	Sauté for 2 minutes total or until opaque throughout.
Large shrimp	Sprinkle with dry brine	0	Brush with oil, smoke for 1½ hours	Sauté for 3 minutes total or until opaque throughout.
Oysters or clams, unshucked	Wet brine	1 hour		Shuck the shellfish, leave on half shell, brush with oil and smoke for 1 hour. No further cooking required.
Mussels, unshucked	Wet brine	1 hour		Simmer in wet brine for 2 minutes or until shells open. Shuck, leave on half shell, brush with oil and smoke for 1½ hours. No further cooking required.

A Good All-Purpose Cure

★ Blend 2 cups brown sugar, 1 cup kosher salt, 3 tablespoons ground mace, 3 tablespoons ground allspice, 3 tablespoons onion powder, 3 tablespoons garlic powder, and 1½ tablespoons ground cloves in food processor for a few seconds. Apply cure generously by rubbing on product by the handful. Cover product with plastic wrap, and refrigerate for 24 hours. Rinse well under running water and dry for 10 to 15 minutes, uncovered, in the refrigerator. Smoke product as usual. Store cure in airtight container. If it hardens, just buzz it again in the food processor for a few seconds.

BRINES AND CURES FOR FISH AND SEAFOOD

Fish and Shellfish Brine

✳ Smoke-cooking, although it has a preserving effect, is not a preserving process. Brining adds to the appearance and flavor of the finished product. Curing in a brine solution reduces moisture content, retards formation of bacteria and enhances flavor. Use a brine of the same strength each time for consistent results. Vary the length of time the product stays in the brine, rather than the strength of the brine.

✳ Tip: An 80 percent salt solution is one that will float a fresh raw egg or potato.

Cookshack Dry Brine Cure

$^{1}/_{2}$ c. table salt
$^{1}/_{2}$ c. sugar or brown sugar
$^{1}/_{4}$ tsp. ground white pepper
$^{3}/_{4}$ tsp. dried thyme
10 lb. poultry, fish or shellfish

✳ Mix first 4 ingredients in a small bowl. For thin fish filets or shrimp, lightly sprinkle the dry-brine mixture over all surfaces of the fish or shrimp.

✳ Note: Dry Brine can also be used for poultry. Sprinkle poultry with a heavy but even coating of Dry Brine, cover with plastic wrap, and refrigerate for length of brining time specified in the Guide to Brining and Smoking (page 176). Wipe off brine. Let poultry stand at room temperature for about 1 hour or until a translucent glaze or pellicle forms on its surface.

Brine One

*Add flavoring ingredients to enhance the flavor of the finished product.
Experiment with dill, dry white wine, ginger, allspice, black pepper, crushed
bay leaves, fruit juices, flavored vinegars, soy sauce, etc.*

4 gal. water
$1^{1}/_{2}$ c. lemon juice
5 lb. noniodized salt
$2^{1}/_{2}$ lb. brown sugar
2 tbsp. liquid onion
2 tbsp. liquid garlic

✳ Soak the fish or shellfish in the brine solution in a nonmetallic container. Brining time varies from 30 minutes for small shellfish to 18 hours for large, whole fish. As a general rule, soak product in brine for 1 hour per pound. When ready to smoke, remove from brine, rinse lightly and allow to dry thoroughly in refrigerator for several hours.

Brine Two

*This brine can be stored in the refrigerator and re-used 3 times, as
long as, each time, it is used to brine only the same type of food.*

Kosher salt
1 large egg
Sugar, brown sugar or honey
10 to 12 lb. fish, shellfish, meat or poultry

✳ Pour 1 gallon cold water into a nonmetallic kettle or bucket. Stir in 2 cups kosher salt. Add the egg, in its shell, to the salted water. If egg does not float, add additional salt 1 tablespoon at a time (keep track of how much salt you add) until egg floats to the surface. Remove egg, then add enough sugar to equal the amount of salt you have already added; stir to dissolve. Add fish, shellfish, meat or poultry of choice. Make sure that the food is submerged. Transfer kettle to the refrigerator. Let stand for brining time specified in the Guide to Brining and Smoking (pages 176–177). Remove fish from the brine; reserve and refrigerate brine for use another time. Let fish stand at room temperature for about 1 hour or until a translucent glaze forms on its surface. Smoke for time specified in the Guide to Brining and Smoking (pages 176–177).
Yield: 1 gallon wet brine.

All-Purpose Cure

1/2 c. table salt
1/2 c. sugar or brown sugar
1/4 tsp. ground white pepper
3/4 tsp. dried thyme
10 lb. fish, shellfish or poultry

✳ Mix first 4 ingredients in a small bowl. For thin fish filets or shrimp, lightly sprinkle the dry brine mixture over all surfaces of the fish or shrimp. Yield: 1 cup cure.

✳ Note: All-Purpose Cure can also be used for poultry. Sprinkle poultry with a heavy but even coating of All-Purpose Cure, cover with plastic wrap and refrigerate for length of brining time specified in the Guide to Brining and Smoking (pages 176–177). Wipe off cure. Let poultry stand at room temperature for about 1 hour or until a translucent glaze or pellicle forms on its surface.

Seafood Cure

1 lb. kosher salt
1/2 oz. Prague powder #1
1 oz. fennel seeds
12 oz. brown sugar
1/2 oz. cloves
1/2 oz. white pepper
1/2 oz. bay leaf
1/2 oz. juniper berries
1/2 oz. allspice
1/2 oz. mace

★ Combine all ingredients in food processor and blend until powdered or until whole spices are ground. Yield: 32 ounces.

Brine

1 c. Seafood Cure
1/2 gal. cold water

★ Dissolve 1 cup of the Seafood Cure in 1/2 gallon cold water.

Dry Cure for Salmon

★ Mix fresh herbs, such as cilantro, basil and tarragon with brown sugar, salt and a little cinnamon or ginger. Rub into salmon. Refrigerate overnight. Next day, scrape off cure and cold-smoke salmon for 45 to 60 minutes.

Smoked Curing Salt for Salmon

2 c. packed brown sugar
1/3 c. pickling salt
1 tbsp. dry mustard
1 tbsp. celery salt
1 tbsp. black pepper
1 tbsp. paprika
1 tbsp. garlic salt
1 tbsp. cayenne pepper
1 tbsp. onion salt

★ Layer salmon skin to skin and meat to meat, sprinkling each layer with curing salt. Marinate for 48 hours. Spray smoker rack with vegetable oil spray. Arrange filets skin down on smoker rack on oiled cheesecloth so that, when filets are removed from rack, the skin will stick to the cheesecloth. Smoke for 4 hours.

SMOKING WOOD

A NOTE ABOUT WOODS:

★ Always smoke with plain, untreated woods. They burn much cleaner than other cooking fuels. Chemical laden briquets produce smoke that is higher in sulphur dioxide, nitrogen oxide and hydrogen sulfide dusts. Chips or sawdust cannot produce the sweet, rich flavor associated with pit barbecue. The flavoring resin burns out of small pieces almost immediately.

HICKORY:

★ Undoubtedly the most popular hardwood, hickory gives that sweet, smoky, flavor traditional in Southern-style cooking. It works well with just about everything. Hickory is recommended for poultry, fish and pork.

MESQUITE:

★ Second in popularity to hickory, mesquite has a stronger woody taste. Though often used for fish steaks it compliments richly flavored meats such as duck, lamb and thick cuts of beef. Mix with hickory to create your own signature taste.

APPLE, CHERRY AND PEACH:

★ These fruitwoods work well with golden-tinged meats like veal and pork, as well as with poultry and game birds. Mix with hickory for a custom wood blend.

ALDER:

★ This wood, used most often in the Pacific Northwest, is fresh and pungent.

BIRCH:

★ This aromatic, slightly resinous wood is used in the upper East and Midwest.

CORNCOBS:

★ Used most often in Vermont and other parts of New England, corncobs produce smoke with a green scent reminiscent of corn.

GRAPEVINE:

★ A European tradition, "grape chips" are available in the United States. With a more delicate flavor than hardwoods, they impart a sweet, winey flavor that is wonderful with fish and poultry. We do not recommend using grapevine unless you are certain that the plants have not been sprayed with pesticide.

SEAWEED:

★ With its tangy smoke flavor, seaweed enhances lobster, crab, shrimp, mussels, clams and all mild-flavored fish. It must be washed and dried in the sun before use.

HERBS:

★ Dried or fresh rosemary, tarragon and basil can be added to the smoker's woodbox for subtle seasoning. Soak in water before adding. Use an aluminum foil "boat" to hold loose or small pieces such as herbs, spices or citrus peel.

GENERAL GUIDELINES FOR WOOD USAGE

★ Dark chickens, with a bitter taste on the skin, are a result of oversmoking, or using too much wood.

★ Small cuts of poultry require a very small amount of wood. Poultry tends to hold smoke on its skin, and too much wood causes a bitter taste. The larger the bird, the more wood you can use. Start with the smallest amount of wood listed on the chart.

★ "Roast beef" without smoke flavor is a result of undersmoking or using too little wood.

★ Poultry and fish require much less wood than beef and pork.

RECOMMENDED WOOD AMOUNTS	
PRODUCT	AMOUNT OF WOOD
Poultry	2 to 6 ounces
Beef	6 to 8 ounces
Pork	4 to 8 ounces
Fish	2 to 6 ounces

★ Your operator's manual specifies the maximum amount of wood that your smoker oven can safely use. Do not exceed this amount. Twenty pounds of wood is enough to smoke approximately 1200 pounds of meat.

Cookshack Inc. is a leading manufacturer of Smoker Ovens. For over 35 years Cookshack has manu-factured state-of-the-art Smoker Ovens used to prepare traditional pit style barbecue and fine smoked foods. Our products are found in restaurants and hotels throughout the U.S., and around the world. Supermarkets, convenience stores, and meat markets also use them to prepare smoked foods for retail sales. About 20 years ago, Cookshack added a line of residential Smoker Ovens to its product line. This cookbook is a collection of recipes from our customers and employees. Most of the recipes have been designed for a Cookshack Smoker Oven, however they can be cooked in any smoker. When using other smokers, simply follow the operation instruction for your smoker to maintain the temperature suggested in the recipes. Some of the recipes are designed for our larger smokers, but can easily be bro-ken down for smaller smokers.

The following is a list of Cookshack models and their capacity:
Series 008—20 pounds of meat
Series 50—30 pounds of meat
Series 100—100 pounds of meat
Series 200—200 pounds of meat
Series 300—300 pounds of meat

Following is a list of accessories for a Cookshack smoker mentioned in the cookbook:
Seafood Grill—small mesh grill for smoking small items. A grill topper will also work.
RibHooks—small hook which allows you to cold smoke in a Cookshack smoker.
Cookshack is one of the few smokers on the market that has this feature.

List of Spice blends and substitute items:
Cookshack Spicy Barbecue Sauce—Traditional Texas-style sauce, KC Masterpiece, etc.
Cookshack Rib Rub—Traditional Pit Style rub, substitute Cain's barbecue spice, etc.
Cookshack Spicy Barbecue Sauce Mix—Spice blend to make Cookshack Spicy Barbecue Sauce, see recipe below for substitute.
Cookshack Spicy Chicken Rub—Traditional Cajun-style rub, substitute Tony Creole's Cajun rub.
Cookshack Chili Mix—Bold chili flavor, substitute William's Chili Mix.

List of difficult items to find:
Achiote paste—Paste made by pureeing annatto fruit.
Bouquet Garni—Fresh herb mixture tied together.
Glace de Vouille—French dry white wine, substitute with any dry white wine.
Grappa—A dry colorless brandy distilled from fermented grape pomace.
Prague Powder—Curing salt with sodium nitrate and red food coloring, substitute Morton's Tenderquick.

Barbecue Sauce Mix:
2 tbs. granulated onion
2 tbs. ground black pepper
2 1/2 tbs. granulated garlic
1 tsp. chili powder
2 tsp. cumin
2 tsp. mustard
2 tsp. ground rosemary
2 tsp. ground thyme

TROUBLESHOOTING

★ If your product does not turn out the way you wanted, or the way you expected, check the chart below for help and try again.

PROBLEM	SOLUTION
Not enough smoke flavor	Increase amount of wood
No smoke ring	Rub with dry curing salt, let stand for 1 hour before smoking, rinse, dry and smoke
Load cooks unevenly	Load according to directions in Operator's Manual with lighter to heavier from bottom to top
Poultry too dark, skin tastes bitter	Decrease amount of wood
Poultry has mushy texture	Dry poultry thoroughly before loading in smoker
Cracked skin on poultry	Rub skin with oil, mayonnaise or salad dressing before smoking or wrap poultry with two layers of cheesecloth and tie with string to hold in place
Ribs not dark enough	Increase amount of wood
Ribs not "falling off the bone"	Increase cooking time to 4 hours; add moisture with Cookshack Water Magazine
Ribs too dry	Increase oven humidity with Cookshack Water Magazine
Brisket is tough	Use untrimmed briskets and increase cooking time or marinate trimmed briskets for 2 hours each side (4 hours total) in sunflower oil before smoking
Vegetables are dark color and bitter tasting	Decrease amount of wood
Fish is not red enough	Add food coloring to brine before brining fish (see To Artificially Color Fish)

INDEX

SAUCES

SHELLFISH & SEAFOOD

SMOKIN' NOTES AND FAVORITE RECIPES

SMOKIN' NOTES AND FAVORITE RECIPES

SMOKIN' NOTES AND FAVORITE RECIPES

SMOKIN' NOTES AND FAVORITE RECIPES

SMOKIN' NOTES AND FAVORITE RECIPES

SMOKIN' NOTES AND FAVORITE RECIPES